HOW TO SOLVE PROBLEMS AND PREVENT TROUBLE

by
Richard W. Wetherill

REVISED EDITION
COPYRIGHT © 1962, 1977, 1991
BY
HUMANETICS FELLOWSHIP
ROYERSFORD, PA 19468

All Rights Reserved

THE ALPHA PUBLISHING HOUSE
677 ELM ST, STE 112
PO BOX 255
ROYERSFORD, PA 19468

ISBN 1-881074-01-3
978-1-881074-01-4

PRINTED IN THE UNITED STATES OF AMERICA

Preface

Many Unnecessary Problems

PRESSURES AND tensions of modern life can be reduced enormously, and the information presented in this book tells how. The information has been and is being tested in daily use by persons from various walks of life.

They all say the information is correct and that it is important.

They tell startling stories of what it is doing for them. They say the information is new, and many of them say they resisted some portions of it at first. The evidence is that no great progress is made except by changing from the old to the new, and the pioneering work of changing is ordinarily resisted at first.

The person who resists is behaving naturally.

If he persists through the initial resistance, however, he makes remarkable discoveries. He becomes aware that problems he thought were necessary are not necessary at all, and he learns how various objectionable conditions in his life can be changed.

Soon he finds that his original resistance is replaced by an eagerness to learn more.

When a person really understands the basic message of this book, he experiences a happiness he had never known.

This book is a kind of behavioral textbook, and while the information is presented on a nonreligious basis, everybody is entitled to seek God as best he can. Many persons say that this book helped them to find God. When understood, it will help people to find desirable objectives of all kinds. The reason is that it removes mental blinders that have kept people living in unsuspected darkness.

The purpose of the chapters that follow is to enable a person to become fully logical, to think more clearly and successfully in all departments of life, and to recognize and understand reality. It will enable him to learn how to identify and drop wrong thinking so that right thinking becomes instinctive.

That is purpose enough for one book.

At first, that purpose may seem rather vague and indefinite because the results take so many forms that they defy any hope of simple description.

Actually describing them seems to involve wild exaggeration.

A selection of results includes the correction of personality flaws and faults earlier not only uncorrectable but some that were undetectable, destruction of bad habits and compulsive misbehavior, elimination of vague feelings of guilt or fear, and even ending susceptibility to various sicknesses and accidents.

If that seems too much to expect, study this book with honesty and an open mind, and you will get some fascinating surprises.

Contents

Preface: Many Unnecessary Problems iii

1. Origin Of Problems And Trouble 1
2. Technique For Solving Problems 23
3. Formula For Preventing Trouble 47
4. Carefully Inspect Your Behavior 61
5. Houseclean Your Emotional Life 76
6. Improve Your Effects On People 90
7. Take Your Brains Out Of Chains 113

Chapter 1

Origin of Problems and Trouble

JOHN IS handsome. His youthful good looks are enhanced by the appearance of intelligence and an attractive personality. He impresses people favorably–but not for very long.

Why not? Because John has an unfortunate tendency to lose his temper whenever he fails to get his own way.

Does he blame his outbursts of temper on himself? Of course not.

He blames it on the people who seem to block him. He has made up his mind that they are goading him and trying to defeat him. He becomes totally illogical whenever the subject is mentioned.

John is mixed up in his mind, and he is not the only one.

It is no secret that human beings are illogical because the evidence abounds on all sides. But it is a secret from each person that in many ways he is illogical himself.

What is more important, he doesn't like to be told so.

You can check that by considering any illogical person you know. No matter how unfortunate the mistakes his illogic compels him to make, you know what would happen if you tried to tell him he is illogical, so you do not try.

That is one of the great mistakes that people should stop making: Everybody is illogical in many different ways, and nobody can easily be told.

There is a strong reason why a person objects to being told. The reason is that he is usually unable to detect what is illogical about his behavior because the evidence is somehow concealed from him.

How that evidence is concealed and what can be done to expose it makes a fascinating and, at times, a shocking story.

In the light of present-day events, it is important to tell that story, because unless the story is told, people will not be able to solve their problems and prevent trouble. Why? Because the vast majority of people's problems and trouble are caused by illogical thinking.

At first, that may seem like an extreme statement, but if you think the matter through, you will presently realize that it is not extreme. You will be given information that will enable you to make astonishing improvements in the way you deal with problems and trouble of every kind.

Readers will be helped by two clarifying definitions.

Define illogical thinking as the kind of thinking that leads to illogical action. Define illogical action as the kind of action that leads to problems and trouble. Under those two definitions, illogical thinking is the kind of thinking that leads to problems and trouble.

It is the kind of thinking a person should learn how to identify and avoid.

Of course, he seldom thinks illogically on purpose because nobody really wants problems and trouble. Nevertheless everybody has problems and trouble, and that makes it clear that everybody is inadvertently illogical.

Because people's thinking is illogical, that does not mean they are stupid.

It means that because of inadvertent illogic a person often aims his attention in a direction that leads to problems and trouble. At such times, the more intelligence he has, the more problems and trouble are likely to result from his efforts.

Another definition will also help.

Illogical action may properly be defined as action that gets some result that is different from the result the person who took the action intended. Often a result that is undesirable.

Consider the following specific example:

A person attempts to back his car out of the garage. He puts his foot on the accelerator and drives headlong into the garage wall, doing extensive damage.

He certainly did not intend to do that.

Because of inadvertent illogic, he put his car into forward gear instead of reverse. It was the wrong thing to do and got a result he neither intended nor wanted. It led to problems and trouble.

That is a fair example of what is meant by illogic.

Everybody is the victim of equivalent illogic on various occasions during his life. He gets into trouble with other people as a result, but most of all, he gets into trouble with himself.

Usually he cannot understand that he caused the trouble.

When he drives his car into the garage wall, he understands that he caused the trouble, because his method of causing the trouble is effectively called to his attention.

In a variety of other situations, he lacks that kind of clear evidence.

Suppose a person is engaged in a running conflict with one of his relatives or associates. Others can see that he is contributing his share to the conflict, but he ignores his contributions and talks only of the contributions made by his opponent.

He won't listen when anyone tries to tell him the conflict is partly his fault.

He is unaware of his contributions and cannot believe that he is partly to blame. The same mental blindness that prevents him from avoiding his part of the conflict also destroys his ability to detect it after it has occurred.

That is what keeps conflicts running at home and on the job.

Each person tries to change his opponent instead of trying to change himself. He could readily change himself if he knew he needed changing and knew how to change, but he cannot really change his opponent. So because he misunderstands the cause, he cannot end the conflict.

That is a fair example of the problems and trouble that result from inadvertent illogic hardly detectable by its victim. The average person gets into much more difficulty of that sort than he supposes and, at first, more than he can easily understand.

When a person does understand how he gets himself into problems and trouble, he tries hard to avoid repeat performances. A person who has paid to have his garage and car repaired after inadvertently driving into the garage wall gives close attention to the proper setting of his gears thereafter.

Unfortunately he cannot similarly guard against other problems and trouble that he does not know were caused by his own illogical thinking and behavior.

II

THERE IS a specific reason why illogical action leads to problems and trouble and gets undesired results. The reason is that ***illogical action always tries to contradict nature in some impossible way.***

That is what makes the action illogical.

Everybody can see the contradiction of nature in an effort to drive a car backward while it is in forward gear, but, in general, no one can see how he is contributing to a conflict that he would like to stop and can't. If he could, he would stop the conflict.

Because he can't, he goes on trying to contradict nature.

Enabling him to understand his own illogical contributions to the conflict puts him in possession of the information he needs. Giving that information to people everywhere will enable them to stop their conflicts as well.

That is what has already happened for persons who have

the information.

Not only does the information apply to the problems of stopping conflicts, but it also applies to every kind of problem caused by inadvertent illogic of any sort.

Consider the following examples:

A person who tries to make himself believe that he can get along on half as much sleep as he needs is trying to contradict nature. He may succeed fairly well for a time, but presently his health will suffer.

A person who believes that seven cocktails make him a better automobile driver is trying to contradict nature. He may wind up in a jail or possibly in a hospital or morgue.

A person who decides he is going to get his way regardless of the feelings of other persons active in a joint endeavor is also trying to contradict nature. He may get his way in certain respects, but in the process, he will do violence to voluntary cooperation.

Ask yourself what might happen if you tried to explain to any of those three persons just what sort of problems and trouble he is inviting. You realize at once that any such effort would be wearing and also probably futile.

That typical reaction brings out an important point.

People suffer from problems and trouble of their own making that they are incapable of blaming on themselves, and the task of enabling them to realize just how they cause their problems and trouble is difficult to perform.

That is the task attempted by this book.

III

THE BASIC obstacle that confronts this book should now be fairly obvious. It must convince the reader that he himself is personally often illogical. In the past the average person has considered that information insulting.

There is nothing personal intended by the information,

and when the person who feels insulted learns exactly what process is responsible for his illogic, he stops feeling insulted.

He starts feeling eager to do something to rectify matters.

In one of its simpler manifestations, the process is easy to explain. Everybody will recognize that he himself has gone through the process many times without understanding the serious consequences.

The following paragraphs describe the process:

Each person has motives that drive him. In his efforts to satisfy those motives, he often encounters resistance. Sometimes the resistance comes from nature, as when he is thwarted by the law of gravity or when he wants tomorrow to come today. Sometimes the resistance comes from another person, as when the other person regards him as dangerously competitive, bossy or otherwise disagreeable.

Those situations in which he is resisted lead to misunderstandings.

The fact that the resistance comes from another person does not mean that nature is left out. It only means that the resistance coming from nature is put into expression through a person.

Obviously every person is a part of nature.

Whether or not the resistance comes through a person, when it becomes overpowering, the result is frustration. The person who is blocked is not able to satisfy his motive.

That is a situation everybody has experienced.

Do not think of it as a situation that happens once in a long time. For the average person, it happens often, and it has been happening ever since his infancy.

Not being able to carry out a motive has an unsuspected effect.

When a person is frustrated in his efforts to satisfy his motives, he tends to rebel and express himself in a burst of emotion. That emotion results from his feeling of rebellion.

What he does or says is less important than **what he thinks.**

Everybody has had many experiences with emotional thinking that results from frustration. He knows that in his emotional thinking he tends to talk to himself, usually not aloud, but he puts his thinking into specific sentences.

Consider the following typical examples:

"No matter what I try to do, it doesn't work out." "I'll force things to go my way." "If I can't get what I want, I'll raise a real fuss." "This is one time I'm not going to let myself get pushed around." "Nobody can make a monkey out of me!"

Anyone can easily expand the foregoing list by making contributions from his own private collection of memories.

The analysis of those sentences is illuminating.

Every sentence is somehow illogical and unrealistic. It puts into words something that no rational person would really support. It suggests illogical action.

Usually the person who forms such a sentence has no real intention of living by it. Even when he has, he soon forgets his outburst.

He assumes that when he calms down his thinking goes back to normal.

A central surprise of this book is that his thinking does not go back to normal. Rather it tends to retain the flavor of the emotional sentences. The difficulty is that the individual thinks in terms of his conscious mind, and he does not allow for his unconscious mind.

When he indulges in a burst of emotional thinking, he drops each rebellious sentence into his unconscious mind. After his thinking has supposedly returned to normal because his emotion has subsided, those sentences remain lodged in his unconscious mind.

Perhaps he changes his conscious mind. Perhaps he tells himself, "I didn't really mean those things."

But that kind of thinking does not change his unconscious mind.

Before a person can get rid of the dangerous effects of the

unrealistic and illogical thinking he does in his moments of emotion, he must know how to change his unconscious mind where his distortions of logic are stored.

That is really the subject of this book.

IV

BEFORE CONSIDERING how to change the unconscious mind from wrong to right, consider the effects of specific sentences that are lodged in the unconscious mind as a result of past emotional thinking.

Those sentences have been accumulating since infancy.

They cover an astonishing range of different subjects. In fact, they cover every subject about which the individual has ever thought in one or more of his moments of emotion. Regarding each of the subjects, those sentences are responsible for subtle changes in his thinking that are undetectable by him.

What happens is that in an outburst of emotional thinking the individual substitutes unreality for reality on the subject of the emotion. For him, the unreality thereafter tends to control.

Consider the next specific example:

Suppose a man in a fit of anger directed toward his wife says to himself, "Someday if she makes me mad enough, I'll kill her!"

There are husbands who have formed such a thought.

Suppose that shortly afterward the husband's temper subsides, and he decides that his wife is not really as bad as he had thought while in his temper.

Therefore, he dismisses the thought.

He decides that he would not dream of murdering his wife, even if she did make him very angry. What he does not realize is the seriousness of those words he has dropped into his unconscious mind. He does not realize that he has changed only his conscious thinking. He does not realize that his unconscious mind still intends to carry out the threat.

The exact words of the emotional thinking determine what his reaction will be under the conditions specified by those words.

In effect, the words have become a command phrase, telling him what to do.

If during ensuing years no similar outburst of temper ever occurs, the husband may live out his life without ever carrying out the threat. But if he ever were to be made "mad enough" under the same emotional conditions, he would tend to execute the command. He would have given himself an urge that may turn out to be disastrous.

Daily we read and hear newscasts about irresistible urges that drive people to commit illogical acts, including murder. Now there is a theory that explains the origin of those urges.

They cause all kinds of trouble: crime, drug addiction, environmental destruction, wars at home and on the battlefield and so on.

The kinds of trouble are determined by the precise words contained in the command phrases that people have fed into their unconscious minds during their moments of emotion.

Some of those command phrases are quite obviously dangerous.

Actually every command phrase is dangerous, because every command phrase replaces reality on the unconscious level of a person's mind. He cannot know that the change has occurred.

Virtually always, he loses all recollection of the command phrase.

Of course, his unconscious mind never forgets, but mere unconscious remembering is not what is dangerous. The dangerous feature of a command phrase is that in the appropriate situations it dictates behavior without the person's realization that anything is amiss.

The reason for that result is worth considering.

Every command phrase becomes an unconscious premise that gets used in the person's routine thinking. It gets mixed in with the premises that are conscious and, therefore, can be checked, but because it is itself unconscious, it cannot be checked.

The command phrase compulsively gets used.

Because every human being is naturally logical in his thinking, a wrong premise that gets mixed in with right premises leads to wrong conclusions. Every conclusion that is drawn from thinking involving even one wrong premise is sure to be as wrong as the premise and in exactly the same way.

That is the explanation of the illogical behavior that is seen on all sides among members of the human race.

From early infancy, everybody has installed many command phrases in his unconscious mind during his moments of emotion. They give him wrong premises on many different subjects, and cause his thinking to produce illogical conclusions that are undetectable as such by him.

A person can easily check those facts by observation.

By remembering the conduct of persons he knows, he can prove to himself that people are often illogical in what they say and do. By remembering his failures in getting people to admit they are illogical, he proves to himself that they are not aware of their deviations from what is logical.

As a result, he recognizes the importance of getting the foregoing information into effective general use.

V

AT THIS point, the basic obstacle to comprehension of this information arises for further attention. It is the obstacle mentioned earlier: The average person is likely to consider the information insulting.

If he does, it is because he misunderstands the information.

When he understands correctly, he sees it as the basis of a release from tensions, from frustrations, from fears, from afflictions of many kinds—even from blame.

The reason should make immediate sense.

A person may be to blame for the rebellious emotion under which he formed his command phrases, but once he has installed them in the recesses of his unconscious mind, he cannot control what they make him do. Why not? Because he has no control over his unconsciously caused compulsions.

Once that fact is recognized, it changes many earlier theories on the subject of behavior.

In a certain literal sense, what a person's command phrases make him do represents only a part of the penalty paid for his earlier mistake. When more people understand that, a vast number of public and private improvements will result. One improvement will be that our penal systems will teach offenders how to correct distortions of logic. Another will be that people will stop blaming one another and start getting rid of the causes of problems and trouble by identifying and releasing the command phrases of their own distortions of logic.

A person who understands the cause-and-effect sequence of distortions of logic sees the mistake of blaming anybody for anything.

He does not even blame himself.

He blames the distortions. He knows that it is a person's command phrases that get him into trouble even by trying to be right.

Everybody needs to recognize that important fact and learn about this new approach to the prevention and solution of behavioral problems.

VI

REALIZATION OF that importance is clarified when a person recognizes the extensive damage resulting from distortions of logic installed in the form of unconscious command phrases.

Step-by-step he can consider how that damage develops.

Starting in early infancy, a child is often rebellious and fearful so that before starting school, he accumulates a vast network of command phrases on an extremely wide variety of subjects.

In childhood, he is usually given discipline by others. If he is intelligent, he adds discipline of his own as he matures. But he cannot ever quite overcome the damage from the command phrases of his distortions of logic.

Whenever he tries hard enough, he can thwart the drive of some unconscious command phrases, but he has to try. Usually he sees no reason why he should try because he has no way to check his logic.

At best, he must work against internal resistance.

He must try to resist temptation. He must curb every urge he knows is likely to lead him into problems and trouble—which is difficult.

He does not succeed as often as he supposes. He knows that he gets into various kinds of trouble, but he usually finds some way of blaming the trouble on something outside himself. He has to. Because he knows nothing of his command phrases, he can find no sensible reason for blaming his own thinking.

Only in unusual cases does a person blame himself.

When he is forced to because the facts of life emphatically call a mistake to his attention, he may try to avoid repeating the mistake. That is what happens when he inadvertently drives into the garage wall, but in other cases, he finds it impossible to make the necessary changes.

Origin of Problems and Trouble

Consider, for example, some prevalent compulsions.

Millions of persons would like to stop smoking or drinking or using drugs but have discovered that despite their decision to stop, they cannot. Millions more would make the same discovery if they tried to stop, but their command phrases tell them not to try.

Therefore, they do not know they are in trouble.

Compulsive smoking, drinking and drug abuse quite obviously are acquired behavior problems. Nobody was born a smoker, drinker or drug abuser.

Nobody intends to become victimized by those compulsive behavior patterns. The compulsions develop subtly as the result of many decisions, and each of those decisions can be stated as a command phrase such as:

"Everyone else smokes; I'll feel out of things if I don't." "I do whatever I feel like doing." "I want to have something to keep my fingers busy." "Smoking makes my work bearable." "When I watch the smoke curl up around my face, I feel dreamy." "Sucking makes me feel comforted."

Such sentences have an illogical and unsuspected control over the person who thought them.

Here are typical command phrases that make a compulsive drinker:

"I have to drown my troubles." "After a few drinks, I forget my problems." "At the end of a day's work, I need some drinks to relax." "A cocktail picks me up when I'm down." "I'm going to do everything I want when I'm old enough."

Reasons to use drugs are found in these command phrases:

"Everybody does drugs to feel better." "With my problems, I need to feel better." "I want to get on the fast track." "A fix helps me handle my job." "Needles don't scare me."

At first a person may think those phrases seem too logical to represent illogical thinking that has gained compulsive control.

Whether a phrase seems logical is not the important point.

What is important is whether the thought has gained unconscious control of thinking and behavior. When the thought is established as a compulsive command phrase, it will be used in an illogical way.

It will cause whatever problems and trouble it suggests.

Often it joins forces with numerous other command phrases to cause a result that borrows something illogical from each. Often it can have the effect of causing various kinds of trouble on different occasions. Often it is originally installed in some situation that may have little or nothing to do with its future use.

"I like to drink all the time" is a phrase that could originally have been formed by a child in relation to lemonade. In later years after he starts drinking cocktails, it may help to make his drinking compulsive. ***Usually compulsive drinking, smoking and drug use result from a very large accumulation of command phrases.***

That is shown by the obvious sequences of cause and effect already cited. But it is shown more powerfully by the fact that when phrases of the sort described are properly detected, they lose their effect, and the compulsive conduct stops without effort.

That same principle has been applied to many kinds of wrong behavior.

At first a person may have difficulty realizing the enormous number of different kinds of problems and trouble that are brought under control by the ability to understand and release the compulsive command phrases accumulated from past emotional thinking.

When analyzed, the range is extensive, and apparently it covers just about every kind of problem and trouble to which any member of society is subject.

There is, however, a limitation.

Identifying and releasing command phrases cannot solve a problem nor end a trouble if irrevocable damage has al-

VII

THAT DAMAGE arises in so many and varied areas of life that it seems pointless to list them. Nevertheless, here is a short list: dangerous driving; criminality; tendency to argue, quarrel or engage in conflict; overeating; inattention, inability to concentrate; feelings of rejection, depression, anxiety, fear; memory loss; sluggishness; insomnia; mental blocks to learning and communication.

All those conditions have been corrected by releasing the compulsive command value of sentences installed in the unconscious mind, using techniques and methods to be explained.

Many of the changes seem miraculous, but only because they were not previously understood.

Surprising to most persons is the beneficial effect of correcting distortions of logic on mental, emotional and physical health. Nothing ordinarily regarded as physical is needed to produce that effect. All that is needed is a certain kind of change in thinking.

The relationship between thinking and health has long been recognized in a general way. Now that relationship is being made specific in easily understandable detail.

VIII

ANYBODY SHOULD be able to see how the command phrases cited earlier, if they gain unconscious control over thinking, could cause smoking, drinking and drug use to be compulsive.

The connection can be made just as clear in relation to health.

Consider the sort of command phrase that causes sickness because it causes behavior that invites sickness.

It might be excessive smoking, drinking, drug use, or it might be a tendency to stay up too late every night or something else already cited. It might also be a command phrase that seemingly does not directly relate to health.

It might be a habit of long hours of overwork without reasonable health precautions. It might be indulgence in peculiar dietary habits or perhaps simple overeating. It might be the excessive weight brought on by overeating. It might be a tendency to worry or indulge in violent outbursts of emotion that invite high blood pressure, ulcers or conditions leading to a heart attack.

Any person who invites physical injury or illness by his illogical thinking easily ends that invitation if he gets rid of the illogical thinking.

Those problems are not basically physical.

Many of them can be counteracted by physical means, at least, up to a point. For example, if a person is unable to sleep because of turbulent thinking, he might get relief by taking sleeping pills. The sensible remedy is to end the turbulent thinking that interferes with his sleep.

No person who understands how to correct distortions needs indefinite dependence on any artificial means of inducing sleep.

The same is true of every other problem caused by wrong thinking.

Correct the wrong thinking that is unconsciously prompted, and the problem ceases to exist. Numerous problems and trouble are really mental in origin, and there is just no sense in trying to control them with counteracting measures.

A certain stigma is attached to the idea of mental problems, but everybody has mental problems. The person who admits it to himself about himself takes a helpful forward step.

Origin of Problems and Trouble

Thereafter, he is free to act on the admission, and he solves problems and prevents future trouble.

A person who takes the position that nothing could be wrong with his state of mind thereby stands between himself and solution of his mental problems. Nothing can be done for him until he stops hiding from reality.

Of course, a person who has mental problems is not necessarily a mental patient, and a person who knows he has mental problems is less likely to become one.

He learns how to solve those mental problems himself.

Gradually he learns the relationship between his unconscious thinking and his physical health. He makes the appropriate changes, and soon he also sees the direct relationship between his unconscious thinking and his mental health. He does not have to try very hard to see that command phrases can have a serious bad effect on mental health.

Consider a few phrases that cause poor mental health: "I can't do anything right." "I don't dare depend on myself." "No matter what I try to do, it always fails." "People have it in for me." "I have more problems than I can solve." "When I get emotional, I just can't think." "I know a lot of things I don't dare admit even to myself." "I'm going crazy, and I can't help it." "The people around me are driving me nuts."

Everybody has done a great deal of thinking of the kind indicated. All that thinking tends to be a burden on him, but a bigger burden is the sort of thinking he can't remember having done.

Everybody has done a large amount of that also.

When emotional thinking is exposed by techniques explained in pages to come, startling things happen. Unconscious burdens are shed and so are conscious burdens-in profusion.

The same is true of a person's emotional health.

Command phrases that indirectly affect emotional health

relate to many different subjects. In fact, every command phrase has a bad effect on emotional health. It requires the individual to hide something from his conscious awareness and to go on hiding it.

Many command phrases directly invite emotional trouble.

"I can't control my emotions" is a suitable example. That statement might easily have originated in a situation where it seemed to apply sensibly, as when a serious emotional blow had just shattered a person's composure. If he formed it in an emotional reaction, the concept assumes command value in situations where it could not logically apply. In those situations the person literally cannot control his emotions.

Other phrases that adversely affect emotional health follow:

"I can't take it." "Life is just too much for me." "I'm at the end of my rope." "I just can't help crying." "Now I'll never have another moment's peace of mind." "I'll try hard never to forget what he did to me." "I can't help being frightened." "I can't get a hold of myself."

Anyone can imagine the sorts of situations in which such thinking might be done. Anyone can remember having done similar thinking, and whoever gets it cleaned out of his unconscious mind enjoys much better emotional health.

He is only changing his thinking and is no more practicing medicine or psychiatry than a person who improves his health by reducing the number of occasions when he crosses the street without looking for oncoming traffic.

IX

THE TECHNIQUE for correcting distortions of logic is not recommended as a substitute for needed medical or psychiatric treatment. It is presented only as a means of changing thinking from wrong to right.

As such, using the command phrase technique often gets

astonishing results.

One result is that a person notices instant changes in his conversation and behavior because the unconscious premises that had made his thinking irrational and unrealistic have been eliminated. Consequently they no longer get used.

The following example explains how it works:

Suppose a person has a large collection of command phrases that have the effect of making him insist on converting every conversation into an argument that he feels he must win.

You may know such a person.

As is the case with every other deviation from sane and sensible behavior, that condition is caused by irrational premises lodged in the unconscious mind, tending to control behavior.

Here are typical command phrases that might be involved:

"I'll prove I'm the smartest person alive." "Nobody can beat me at anything." "The winner always gets the prizes." "Everybody keeps trying to prove I don't know what I'm talking about." "Unless I really get steamed up, I can't talk at all." "I can't agree with anybody."

Perhaps that would be a sufficient number of phrases to detect and release in order to change an argumentative person. If more must be detected to get the complete change, then he will benefit by doing the additional amount of necessary work.

After all the relevant command phrases are picked up, the person who formerly had to turn every conversation into an argument and then win the argument would be entirely uninterested in continuing that behavior.

He just wouldn't have the necessary urges.

The same is true in every area of life, whether a problem relates to a person's thinking, conversation, behavior or health.

The compulsive smoker is able to stop smoking. He doesn't have to try to stop. He just loses interest in smoking. While he feels no aversion to smoking, he finds it unattractive and unnecessary. He makes no high resolves against it. He just stops and that's that.

The same is true of a person with any other kind of compulsion.

Gone is his need for resolutions. Gone is his need for pills or treatments of any kind. Gone is his need for self-restraint.

The individual becomes able to do what he had often erroneously assumed he could do. He becomes able to use his brain to intelligently instruct his body. But in order to get that result, he must first correct the distortions of logic that actuate him from unconscious levels.

He cannot successfully contradict those distortions by telling himself counteracting command phrases.

If he tries, he will generate internal resistance. He may find the resistance appearing in the form of tension or effort. He may find his compulsions showing up in some other form as when a smoker stops smoking by turning to candy which increases his weight.

The effort to contradict urges toward wrong behavior is made unnecessary by making the needed changes in unconscious thinking so that the person can behave as he should.

Results in relation to physical health are often amazing.

Certainly nothing is more physical than overweight. Today most persons agree that overweight results from overeating. Despite that fact, millions of overweight persons are unable to reduce, because they cannot drop their compulsions to overeat.

Many of them are well aware of the fact that what they need is a change of thinking, but even with that realization, they cannot change.

When they learn to find and drop the distortions of logic they installed during moments of emotional, unrealistic thinking, they get their appetites under control.

They do not need to count calories, depend on exercises, follow special diets, swallow pills intended to suppress their appetites. They are able to eat what they want, but they do notice various differences in the food they want and the quantity they eat.

They also notice that their weight decreases.

If overweight has the adverse effect on longevity that is widely advertised, the person who brings his weight down to normal presumably also lengthens his life.

In addition he reduces the likelihood that he will need medical attention for the various illnesses and problems brought on by overweight.

That is not the only way he can improve his physical health.

After he discovers what he can accomplish by changing his unconscious thinking, he may decide to deal with other health problems more directly.

Some of his command phrases directly invite sickness.

"I want to be sick, so I can stay home from work." "I'm going to have something wrong, so people will take care of me." "Unless I get my way, I'll take to my bed and be sick."

Some command phrases call for a sickness that is considered to be incurable.

"I want to go to bed and never get up again." "My situation is absolutely hopeless." "Nothing can be done for me." "I can't go on fighting for my life."

People's experience with this information suggests that no physical illness is hopeless.

Astonishing corrections of supposedly incurable diseases have sometimes occurred as a result of using the procedures discussed here. No claim is made that any such corrections can or will be repeated. However, a person who is sick is certainly justified in trying to improve his thinking and to get a correction if he can.

If he tries to apply the appropriate procedure, he may be startled by what happens just as a result of unthinking wrong thoughts. He is much less startled if he already understands the thinking by which people have inadvertently been inviting their problems and trouble.

Chapter 2

Technique for Solving Problems

WHAT HAPPENS when a person installs a distortion of logic in one of his bursts of emotional thinking can perhaps best be described by saying that he catches himself in a mental trap from which he cannot escape by any ordinary process of thought.

Consider the nature of that mental trap.

A person's emotional thinking is physical as well as abstract. Thinking occurs in the physical brain. The electronic impulses of thinking move along electronic circuits composed of brain cells that establish contact with each other for that purpose.

Repeated thinking of exactly the same kind may require no new circuits, because the old circuits remain intact ready for use in every situation where they apply.

Every sudden reaction involves use of old circuits.

When a person sits on a tack, he says, "Ouch!" and rises before he has time to decide what has happened. Only afterward does he collect the pertinent facts, and then only because he has received signals telling him on the conscious level about what has happened.

The same thing occurs when the circuit containing a distortion is used.

The reaction is sudden and automatic. It is not planned and intentional. Usually it does not call attention to itself in any way. It just makes the individual behave irrationally in accord with his command phrases without his awareness that anything is amiss.

The foregoing explanation of the thinking process is based on common knowledge taught to school children as long as fifty years ago. It forms the basis of a logical explanation by which a person of ordinary education and intelligence can understand the process of installing a distortion of logic in the physical sense.

Start at the beginning of the process.

A person's emotion is the force behind his thinking. As the response to an emotional stimulus, he starts formulating ideas, some of which lead to action. Sometimes the action succeeds, and in that case it is logical action.

When a person's action succeeds, it satisfies the emotion that stimulated the thinking and prompted the action. Therefore, the emotion subsides. The purpose of that emotion, among other things, is to close connections between nerve cells in the brain so that thinking can travel along electronic paths in the circuits used to effectuate the desired action. When the emotion subsides, those connections open and are available to form new connections.

In cases of quick, seemingly instinctive action such as exclaiming and suddenly rising after sitting on a tack, the circuits remain closed. Or at least sufficiently closed that they carry the electronic force in the appropriate situations without having to form the connections by means of conscious thinking at the time of the action.

That is a normal, natural procedure.

In cases of illogical thinking that prompt wrong action, a somewhat different procedure is used, and it will be described next.

Illogical thinking is previously defined as thinking that does not succeed in getting a result that satisfies the emotional desires of the person who does the thinking. Therefore, a wrong result does not satisfy the emotional force that stimulated the illogical thinking. Because that emotional force is not satisfied, the emotion does not fully subside. Therefore, the connections between brain cells formed to effectuate the thinking do not unform. They remain for repeated use on future occasions when the same emotion is restimulated.

They produce behavior as compulsive as the action of exclaiming and rising after a person has sat on a tack.

Consider the earlier example of the man who told himself about his wife, "Someday if she makes me mad enough, I'll kill her!"

Those words represent a burst of illogical, wrong thinking done in a flash of emotion. They cannot lead to action that satisfies the emotion behind them unless their command is executed. Therefore, the words of that command are trapped in a closed mental circuit that cannot be reopened by any ordinary process of thought.

The command to act waits for the day of specific restimulation.

The restimulation may never occur, but if his wife ever happens to enrage him in the precise way necessary to cause an upsurge of the same emotion, the husband will murder her as surely as he will exclaim and suddenly rise after he has sat on a tack.

II

BECAUSE EACH person has done a large amount of emotional thinking, each person has many closed mental circuits inviting trouble of various kinds. When the trouble arises, he faces the problem of dealing with it. Basically there is only one way to put a stop to recurring trouble.

He must reopen the closed mental circuits that send his thinking compulsively through the illogical, wrong patterns set up when the individual first did the emotional thinking inviting the trouble.

Anybody can reopen his closed mental switches, but he

has to know how.

Of course, he cannot reach into his brain with his hand and physically open or close mental switches so that the results of his past emotional thinking are eliminated, but he can throw the necessary switches in a physical sense just by using a thinking process.

Nobody can think consciously without throwing mental switches. He forms and unforms them all the time. His difficulty in relation to his past emotional thinking is that he doesn't throw the proper switches because he doesn't know he should. And also because even if he did know he should, the process of doing it, at first, goes against his inclinations.

The reason is that the individual has strong urges to gratify his unconscious thinking. He does not have an impulse to change it. Until he gets that impulse, he is helpless.

A purpose of this book is to give him that impulse.

When he understands the precise nature of emotional thinking and what it does to him, he gains an intent to do something to rectify the situation in which he finds himself. That causes him to learn whatever he must learn to extricate himself from the predicament he has not known he is in. As he gains understanding, the impulses necessary to lead him toward correction take form and actuate him.

III

THE PURPOSE of those impulses is to locate, identify and release in succession all the closed mental circuits that are causing illogical, wrong thinking and behavior to be compulsively repeated.

Obviously, that is not how problems are ordinarily approached.

Because the person who has problems has not known about his distortions of logic, he tends to blame his problems on factors other than their true cause. Instead of changing his own thinking, he usually tries to change the people and conditions around him. Often that may seem to succeed, although actually it never does.

Consider the explanation of why it fails.

Suppose a person has done emotional thinking that leaves him with an assumption that he cannot get along with his wife. Thereafter he is miserable in her presence. After enough additional emotional thinking, he decides to leave her. Separated from her, he may feel that he has solved his problem, but actually he has only rearranged his life to let him ignore the problem.

There are many other illustrations that could be cited.

Suppose a person forms command phrases telling him he cannot eat certain foods. Seemingly he can solve his problem by eliminating the foods named in those command phrases. But actually his problem is not solved until he rids himself of the command phrases that cause him to be unable to eat those foods. As has been proved by many experiments, correcting distortions enables a person to solve food problems and permits use of rational eating habits.

The same corrections occur when this information is applied in other areas of life.

Suppose a person has command phrases telling him that he is unable to do a certain kind of work. In that case he may assume he has no problem if he successfully manages to avoid such work. Suppose a person has command phrases telling him he cannot take certain action that is really essential to his life. If that happens before he knows how to correct distortions of logic, death could result—unless the problem of counteracting his command phrases is somehow solved.

The usual problem-solving methods in common use seldom do more than counteract a person's command phrases.

There are innumerable ways of counteracting command phrases available. One way is to use the power of contradicting motives. For example, if someone has distortions telling him to criticize his boss, he can use the power of motives to keep his job as a means of holding himself in check. Probably those motives will work well enough that by restraining himself he can keep his job, but only if he avoids too frequent emotion strong enough to override his self-restraint. Whether or not he succeeds depends on the strength of the motives to keep his job in contrast with that of the motives to criticize his boss.

A person's tendency to use artificial means of counteracting the drives that result from past emotional thinking is easily illustrated in the field of medicine.

Stresses of modern life often seem to be the cause of a person's inability to remain alert while at work. Therefore, millions of persons prop themselves up with pep pills, coffee and other more drastic stimulants. There is no doubt that the stimulants do have some of the desired effect, but it is also true that the stimulants can be eliminated with no sense of loss if the distortions are corrected that translate the difficulties of life into unreasonable dullness and fatigue.

Those distortions might have the following command phrases:

"Everything bothers me." "I can't stand this pace." "No matter what I do, I can't wake up until noon." "I need something to prop me up." "I need my bottle to stay alive." "I can't function without a fix."

At first glance it may appear that the foregoing phrases are normal reactions to a life of stress, but that is not the case. Each of those sentences is formed in a moment of real or imagined stress, perhaps in childhood, and each then becomes an irrational rule of life. Analysis of the command phrases quickly shows that none of them is logical.

For example, the statement "Everything bothers me" is not true for the person who formulates it. There are certain things in his life that do not bother him: Sports, getting dressed, eating a meal and so on. Putting that phrase into his unconscious mental circuits gives him an unconscious obligation to live in accord with it.

Therefore, he must react to everything as though he is bothered.

He is in a really difficult situation. He cannot solve his problem by moving away from a source of irritation, because everything will bother him wherever he goes. He may feel inclined to seek pleasures with great determination because sufficiently keen pleasures, at least, tend to dull the edge of his emotional discomfort.

Many persons avidly seek all sorts of pleasures and balms for that reason. They do not solve their problems, because they are always seeking something they never quite succeed in finding.

They cannot solve their problems until they learn to correct the distortions of logic that cause them.

Because people have lacked knowledge of how to do that, they have done the best they could in a world filled with emotional stress. Increasingly they have tended to rely on balms and diversions of one sort or another. In recent years people have used mood-altering drugs. No doubt the drugs do take the edge off some of the unpleasant emotion, but drugs do not cure anything caused by illogical conscious or unconscious thinking. In fact, the drugs allow thinking to go further and further off the track as more distortions are installed, because the effects of conscious and unconscious wrong thinking are made more bearable by a person's drugged state.

When a problem is caused by wrong thinking, there is only one way for a person to solve it.

He has to drop the illogical, wrong thinking.

He should not try to counteract it by resisting the urges it generates or by taking contradictory action. Those procedures cause the problem to become more and more serious as time passes. Instead, he should take action that has the effect of reopening the closed mental circuits that constitute the physical embodiment of the past emotional, unrealistic, illogical, wrong thinking.

IV

THERE IS no use trying to open those closed circuits directly, because the appropriate circuits cannot be located directly.

A person has to take indirect action.

That explains why people are virtually unable to face disagreeable truth about themselves. The disagreeable truth tends to be concealed in their distortions of logic. No matter how the individual tries to face such truth, he cannot succeed.

Asking him to try causes him additional frustration.

You may be able to see how another person is causing himself some kind of trouble, but if he were able to see it himself, he would not stay in the trouble. Asking him to look at that reality or truth is like asking him to lift himself by his bootstraps.

He cannot face the appropriate reality or truth until he has first destroyed the distortions of logic that conceal it, because reality and truth are superseded by his command phrases.

That is the nature of a person's mental trap.

So long as a person retains a distortion, he is blind to truth on the subject of that distortion. In effect, he would rather die than face that truth. After the distortion is released, he need not be asked, because he faces that truth without even trying.

V

A PERSON cannot face concealed truth directly because his distortions stand in the way. Therefore, he must face that truth indirectly. His logical procedure is to face the

Technique for Solving Problems

words of untruth that make up his distortions of logic and release them.

When he does that, their influence on his thinking is gone.

A person is not dominated by a command phrase of which he is aware and knows is illogical. Therefore, he should raise the words of his illogical command phrases to the conscious level where they can be recognized for what they are.

It is important that he find the exact concept.

Unless he does, his mind cannot be freed from the distortion, because the words correctly duplicate the original thinking. In that situation, he sends the necessary electronic force through the same mental circuit that had remained closed ever since the original unrealistic thinking was done.

The words that describe the wrong concept are the key to his release.

All that is necessary is to give those words brief conscious attention without emotion of the sort that accompanied the original illogical thinking.

If he gives attention to his command phrases with that sort of emotion, he simply perpetuates the distortion.

What a person needs is a willingness to give up the concept expressed in the words of the command phrase. Freedom from emotion enables him to accomplish that, and he can achieve freedom from emotion in various ways.

One way is to remain calm while inspecting the words.

Another way may make more sense to a beginner. He should inspect the words with a willingness to see how they are illogical and wrong. Nobody retains a distortion after he sees that it aims in a wrong direction toward action that will frustrate him.

Often the beginner assumes that he should feel a sudden emotional reaction or a sense of great illumination when a distortion is corrected. At times, he may feel a sudden release of tension, but usually the change is hardly noticeable.

He has to make enough corrections that they begin to show in his daily life before he becomes convinced that something important is really happening to him.

Some persons get that result quickly. Because every distortion is installed in an instant, it is also corrected in an instant if it is corrected at all. It is a person's conscious recognition of the command phrases of the distortion that works.

When he understands the process, he corrects distortions as fast as he is able to think of command phrases, and he can think of them in quick succession in relation to most problems he tries to solve.

The whole job is done by releasing his wrong thinking.

Until he acquires skill in using the technique, his distortions seem to hide from him. He cannot approach them directly anymore than he can directly approach the truth they conceal, so he approaches them indirectly.

That is why people did not learn sooner to straighten out their illogical thinking accumulated from the past. The necessary process is different from procedures usually taught because it necessitates thinking about something that tends to elude their minds.

The needed technique is one that enables a person first to bring the elusive ideas into focus, and there are certain ways to accomplish that.

VI

PERHAPS THE easiest form of the technique a person can use is to collect on paper a selection of strong ideas.

He can select any subject at random on which he has strong feelings and put those ideas on a sheet of paper as fast as they come to mind. Each sentence should express the idea exactly–just as he has often expressed his feelings to himself or others over the years.

Perhaps he may select the name of some person he dislikes. If so, he should write the name of that person at the top of his paper, and then list exactly what he has thought about that person in the past.

He should not edit the list nor make it seem polite.

He should write down exactly all the uncomplimentary, critical remarks he has made to himself and others about the person involved.

The following sentences are typical:

"He's the most dishonest person I've ever met." "I couldn't trust him with anything." "He's always trying to get me into trouble." "If I had my choice, I'd never speak to him again." "The sight of him makes me sick at my stomach." "He gives me a pain in the neck."

Those sentences may seem extreme at first glance, but they are just typical of the thinking everybody does at various times in his life. There are some people who do it virtually all the time.

It is illogical and wrong for a person to form those judgments, because they stick in his mind and influence his attitudes. If he thinks about those sentences in relation to any person he knows and happens to dislike and analyzes the sentences carefully in complete honesty, he will see that they make little real sense.

Any brain infested with such sentences in relation to other persons is a brain in chains.

Those judgments impair a person's effective intelligence and make him compulsively antisocial toward anybody he dislikes.

For example, books on getting along with people usually advise people to see the best in others. But anyone who has installed the foregoing distortions in relation to other persons is sure to see them through those distortions, and he certainly could not see the best in them.

He would be mentally blinded to their virtues, and that mental blindness would remain until the distortions were corrected. No change is needed in the other person to correct the distortions. The change is needed in the person who has them.

After he corrects the distortions, he can see virtues. More important, his mind is no longer trapped by the unrealistic thinking that magnified every fault and manufactured faults where no faults existed. In short, his thinking becomes rational and free flowing.

The way a person gets corrections is to inspect his distortions.

After he accumulates perhaps two dozen samples of strong thinking about the person he dislikes, he should pause to consider them. He should seek flaws in the logic they express. When he finds illogic in a sentence, he has released its power to dominate his thinking thereafter.

He may think some sentences seem logical even under close inspection.

For example, a person may be willing to admit that it is illogical to think "He is lower than a worm," but perhaps refuse to budge on "He makes me sick." In that case he just has to go on getting sick periodically until he is willing to let go of that thought.

If he has to associate closely with the person about whom he has that distortion, he may have some chronic illness as a result of his determination to retain the illogical thought.

That may not become serious if he continues using the technique for correcting distortions.

After a person goes far enough that he really understands what a distortion is and how it afflicts him, he is glad enough to release every distortion no matter how warmly he has cherished it in the past. Therefore, he should continue working on his list, crossing off the items he sees are illogical.

After the first inspection of the list, he should extend it and add more items. At first, he can draw on his memory, and after he exhausts his memory, he can draw on his imagination.

Technique for Solving Problems

There is solid reason why that is effective.

Many of a person's most serious distortions were installed long ago. He cannot consciously remember ever having thought them or having put them into spoken words. Therefore, they are beyond his conscious recall.

The phrases he remembers thinking are easy to capture. But the phrases that have dropped out of conscious recall are also possible to capture by the process of drawing on imagination.

If a person considers the matter, he can see why.

A person's imagination tends to follow paths already established. If he has ever thought a command phrase, he can think of it again. Actually he can think of it more easily than he could think of a new phrase. Therefore, when he draws on imagination to extend his list, he tends to include all the pertinent phrases that would otherwise be out of reach.

Presently he starts recognizing some of those phrases.

By using imagination to extend his memory, he gradually enables himself to stretch his memory. Whether or not he consciously recognizes all the command phrases is not important. What is important is to get all the pertinent phrases into the list and see how they are illogical and cause compulsive behavior.

Some of them will have a strong grip on his emotions.

When he has that difficulty, a variation in the technique is suggested to help him get started.

Under that variation, in addition to looking at each phrase to see how it is somehow illogical and unrealistic, he should notice his emotional reactions. If he still feels strongly about a sentence, he should keep it in the list; then go over the list daily to add a few items. In review, he should also look for former items that no longer arouse his emotions. Those are the items to cross out.

As long as a command phrase arouses a person's emotions, it can be assumed that he is not yet released from .its power to control him.

If the process of giving daily attention to his list is continued, he presently discovers that he has no items left to add or cross off. He also discovers that he no longer harbors those former ill feelings.

If he applies the same treatment to his thinking in relation to every person he dislikes, he presently finds he is unable to think of anybody he dislikes. He will not have changed anyone except himself, but the others will all seem different to him.

As a person realizes the significance of the changes he has made in himself, he also begins to realize the significant results that can be accomplished by using the same procedure wherever it applies.

Instead of limiting the procedure to dealing with animosities, he applies it to other problems also. Perhaps a variety of situations he dislikes. To his surprise, he may discover that in a short time he can change his thinking about many of those situations, too.

VII

THE USUAL approach to a disagreeable situation is very different from the procedure just described. In the case of animosity, for example, the usual approach is either to retaliate or else to avoid the person disliked.

A person using either of those approaches never really solves the problem of his animosity.

When a problem is caused by illogical, wrong thinking trapped in closed mental circuits, the only way to solve the problem is to reopen those closed mental circuits.

The procedures that have been described have that effect as they throw the precise mental switches that need to be thrown.

There are other variations of the technique that may seem more direct.

VIII

NO VARIATION of the technique is really direct. The reason is that by direct approach to a distortion, the individual guarantees that he will merely act on it instead of correcting it. The indirect approach enables him to inspect it.

As soon as he inspects it honestly, he drops it.

No distortion of logic can stand honest inspection by its victim, and he remains its victim only so long as he fails to inspect it with the intent to do the right thing.

When a person starts listing his strong ideas on paper, his direct effort is not so much to inspect those ideas as to express them. In that situation he is acting in accord with his distortions in a harmless way, with the result that he puts his distortions where he can see them.

If he applies the procedure correctly, he has a tendency to feel that he is not listing distortions but is instead listing ideas that he feels are justified. In fact, the more logical he thinks a strong idea will appear under analysis, the more reason he should include it. He later will discover that many ideas he had long considered logical cannot stand the light of rigorous analysis.

By the procedure of writing strong ideas, the indirect approach is effectively illustrated.

After a person really understands distortions and the process of approaching them indirectly, he clearly sees how they have led him into problems. He sees why he has difficulty counteracting those problems and why he could never really solve them. He sees how to use the indirect approach in various ways.

Always the indirect element should be preserved.

No matter how much a person knows about distortions of logic, he cannot look at a distortion directly until after he has released it. That information also applies to distortions that he accumulates in a written list.

At first each command phrase seems like a realistic thought instead of an unrealistic, wrong thought. The individual believes that he is writing truth rather than untruth. But hidden under each distortion is the truth that it conceals, and that truth does not become visible until the distortion is released.

When does the release occur?

It occurs at the precise instant when the illogic of the command phrase is detected. Thereafter, it no longer deludes.

Because every distortion deludes the individual, the process of locating distortions can be difficult. At first he does not know where to look, because he has no consciousness of having distortions. At first, he may not be able to find any.

It is important for him to learn how and where to look.

If he is fortunate enough to know some person who understands distortions and how they work, he can be given help provided he is willing to accept it. In the beginning that sort of help is hard to accept until the individual has so much competence in correcting distortions that his need for help is greatly reduced.

Consider how such help works.

Suppose a person sees someone who has distortions on the subject of overeating. That is easy. There are many such people and they are identifiable by their size.

If he observes their behavior, he can see their distortions getting used. He can infer the distortions from their behavior and hear them being expressed in ordinary conversation.

People constantly voice their distortions.

By watching people's behavior, a person can accumulate a list of command phrases for persons he knows. By listening to what they say, he can extend the list, especially by listening to what they say with strong emotion. When anyone expresses himself with strong emotion, he is almost always voicing one or more of his command phrases.

After a person learns enough about somebody else's distortions, he may be able to tell why he suffers from the problem of overweight.

Here are typical phrases causing overweight:

"I have to be eating all the time." "When I'm not eating, I just worry." "If I can't eat what I want, life isn't worth living." "I have to eat or I'd starve to death." "I care more about my appetite than my weight." "Nothing can stop me from eating!" "I'd hate to be skinny." "The smell of food makes me hungry."

The person who has those phrases may try hard to reduce but finds he is blocked. If he restrains his appetite by great effort over a period, as soon as he relaxes the effort, he tends to regain the weight he lost.

The person who understands about distortions of logic knows why, but he cannot easily tell someone who does not.

If that person understood distortions, he would know what to do about his overweight. If he doesn't understand distortions, he tends to resist being told.

Although he tries to counteract the promptings of his various command phrases, he resists having them pointed out to him. If his attention is called to one of them, he tends to become indignant or defensive.

He may deny the command phrase. Denying it merely holds it intact, but that is not the only way of holding it intact. He can do it with a reaction exactly opposite to denying it.

He may agree with the command phrase.

If he is told, "You have to be eating all the time," he may say, "Yes, I do. That's just my trouble!" In that instance he destroys his chance to get released from the wrong thought.

Neither of those two reactions is a logical response.

His logical response is to recognize that his thinking is incorrect, that a command phrase should always be dropped and that if he denies or agrees with it, he is supporting his compulsion to overeat.

Obviously he cannot give that response unless he understands distortions of logic.

People who do understand are able to provide enormous help to one another as they work their way out of hidden mental traps. But at the outset, a person may have to work alone.

Therefore, what has been said about detection of distortions in another person has been said mainly for illustration.

When a person attempts to detect a distortion in someone else, he benefits by the fact that he can easily be indirect in his approach. He also benefits by the fact that he can learn to recognize his own distortions even if he approaches them directly, provided he does not have identical distortions. In that case he cannot recognize them in another person.

Why is that? Because every expression of that distortion seems logical to him. He is blocked from recognizing its illogic as effectively as in the case of directly seeking distortions in himself.

His observation of distortions in other people's conversation and behavior offers great value in his efforts to release his own intelligence. By observing others he can learn valuable lessons about how to detect similar distortions in himself.

For example, he can learn how a person looks and sounds when he is acting under the promptings of his command phrases. Those observations enable him to notice the words of the person's command phrases by analyzing his actions. He can decide how a person's tone of voice is influenced when he is putting one of his command phrases into specific words.

Then he can apply all that sort of information to himself.

Gradually he learns to recognize the emotional symptoms that tell him when he is in danger because he is thinking through distortions. He can think back at once to what he was saying or doing and try to remember his thinking at the time.

From his behavior he can infer the wording of command phrases. His ordinary conversation is also revealing. Often he will be able to isolate command phrases just by remembering what he said, especially with strong feeling. His thinking is even more revealing.

When under emotion, a person thinks in terms of command phrases–those he already has on the unconscious level and those he newly forms.

Everything he thinks, says and does expresses command phrases while actuated by emotion. The difficulty is that he seldom supposes he is so actuated. Therefore, learning to notice it in others is important.

Whatever he learns in relation to them, he can apply to himself.

IX

SUPPOSE A person has learned that talking under emotional strain is an indication that he is expressing distorted thinking. Suppose he has identified emotional strain by observing it in others. If so, next time he detects such emotional strain in himself he can take time out to analyze what he was just saying.

Under careful analysis, he will detect flaws in it by recognizing command phrases.

Every time he does, he corrects distortions. More important, he trains himself to be alert to what he says. Presently he discovers that sometimes he is able to detect and release a distortion before he puts his command phrases into words.

That procedure saves him from the consequences of that particular expression of irrational conversation.

Suppose you have learned from the foregoing information that when people around you get into trouble, it is because they have taken illogical action. If so, you can put that information to good use in relation to yourself.

When you get into trouble of any kind, you can think about the distortions that led you into the trouble. Instead of blaming factors outside yourself and trying to change them, you are able to put attention on the real cause of the trouble: command phrases of distortions of logic.

Suppose you have learned how to translate someone else's conversation and behavior into the command phrases that caused it. If so, you can similarly analyze your own conversation and behavior.

You can think back to various situations in which you encountered results that were wrong and unwanted. Remember what you said and did. Look for command phrases you may have expressed in your conversation and behavior. Use the same indications that you have learned to detect by studying the conversation and behavior of others.

In doing so, you apply the indirect approach to yourself.

X

THERE IS a way of using the indirect approach that gives it almost the effect of a direct approach, and many persons are using it. While it requires skill and the confidence of experience to make it really effective, it is a quick method.

It is known as the command phrase technique.

Every distortion of logic can be described in command phrases that cause an unending series of problems. Those problems can be counteracted, but they cannot be solved except by correcting the thinking that causes them.

Therefore, a person should begin with the recognition of a problem.

Any problem will serve, although he is wise to begin with some problem he has reason to suspect was caused by his own wrong thinking. If he is honest about it, he can identify several such problems with little effort.

Perhaps he has difficulty going to sleep when he should.

Selection of the problem provides his lead and gets him started. He may select the problem at a time when he is suffering from it. Therefore, if he goes after command phrases that keep him from falling asleep, probably he is lying in bed at the time keenly aware of the problem.

In that situation nothing is lost and something is to be gained by applying the technique. He may as well give his insomnia proper attention and get rid of it.

Giving the problem proper attention is certainly more interesting than counting sheep.

He should ask inside his mind what command phrases could have the effect of keeping him awake. He may remember various statements he has made on the subject of his sleeplessness. He can use his imagination to get more phrases. Presently command phrases come to his mind almost effortlessly.

Some of them he may mistakenly consider too logical to be command phrases.

For example, if the command phrase is "I just can't sleep no matter how I try," he can easily delude himself into imagining that the phrase merely describes a condition that exists.

In the first place, he has to recognize that his troublesome sleep pattern is a solvable problem.

The fact is that the foregoing quotation involves a sentence that was not logical at the time it was originally thought. It was probably formed in exasperation, and it was incorrect. Many times afterward, that person did sleep. That fact alone proves that he was wrong when he said, "I just can't sleep no matter how I try."

The sentence was not logical then, and it is still not logical. Even if he repeats it to himself many times in the exasperation of sleeplessness, it will still not be rational. After he gets tired enough, he will fall asleep. Therefore, he should not delude himself by that statement any longer. By detecting its illogic, he releases its hold on his mind.

That correction lets him cancel one reason for staying awake.

He can apply the same procedure to one command phrase after another so long as he remains awake. The phrases most likely to come to his mind are the ones that are keeping him awake. He can give each just enough attention to recognize it as a command phrase, and presently he will fall asleep.

He may reach a permanent solution for his problem of sleeplessness in his first effort, but if not, no matter. Whenever he finds himself unable to fall asleep, he can try again, and by that procedure he will eventually get rid of all the responsible phrases. He shouldn't be surprised if there are dozens of them, because he has spent a lot of hours forming them while he courted sleep perhaps for many years. All that mental rubbish must be disposed of before the problem is completely solved.

His sleep problem can be solved in just a small part of the time he formerly spent wrestling with it.

So it is with every other kind of problem. If a problem is serious enough to demand attention, it is serious enough to solve rather than to go on trying to counteract it. He can just use the time and attention he already gives the problem to get rid of it.

Doing that with one problem after another gets startling results. Perhaps a person won't see those results in the first day or week, but some persons report desired changes at once.

To get started, a person should make a list of problems to work on.

At first he may overlook many of his serious problems, but no matter. In due course they will come to his attention. A person's problems should be approached in the order in which they come to his attention so that they can be dealt with as a matter of course while he goes about his daily affairs.

In the process he is often astonished by the degree of control over his life and bodily functions that is attributable to distortions.

The following is a list of the problems others have eliminated:

Boredom, restlessness, impatience, quick temper, shyness, self-consciousness, talking without thinking, elimination of bad habits, inability to concentrate, tendency always to be in a hurry, emotional tension, inclination to worry, feelings you must make every decision and cannot ever depend on the decisions of others, sour relationships, physical ills and accidents.

There is no problem likely to be mentioned that does not belong in the list in one form or another, but a beginner should not arouse initial skepticism by selecting problems he considers impossible to solve. There are several problems in that list a person could expect to do something about.

As he makes progress, he will get many interesting surprises.

He will detect problems where he thought no problems existed. He will discover that human beings do an enormous amount of needless suffering of many different kinds. As a result of that discovery, he will also change the course of his life.

The average person advances from one frustration to another and tends to consider it normal. He has to get up when he would rather stay in bed. He has to go to bed when he would rather stay up. He tries to get solace from balms that fail to satisfy. He does all sorts of things because he has to, and he refrains from all sorts of things because he must. That makes his life difficult.

Every frustration he encounters, he should realize, points to an example of illogic.

He can pause to think and ask himself what sort of illogical thinking invited the frustration. He can pick up command phrases and get as many as he easily can. If the needed changes elude him, he should repeat the procedure and continue until the desired change occurs.

As he progresses, he finds that his life simplifies.

Gradually he discovers that life is not so complicated as people are fond of saying. It is the mechanisms of life that are complicated, and the purpose of those complicated mechanisms is to enable people to simplify their lives. Unfortunately people devise their own complexities, but with understanding, they can be eliminated.

By using the command phrase technique, a person sees remarkable improvements in his mental, emotional and physical health.

Those improvements are happening to the persons who are engaged in a research project for that purpose.

They know that every phrase of illogical thinking places an added strain on the person who harbors it and that each phrase causes illogical behavior and hence frustration. Those results also increase his tension, because many phrases demand action that interferes with a rational way of life. In addition, many phrases directly invite poor health by their wording.

Consider the following command phrases:

"My father died of a heart attack, and so will I." "Whenever a bug starts going around, I'm always one of the first to catch it." "I just know I'll die from some virus." "It's normal for me to be sick every few months." "I'm sick of my job."

Maybe you can't believe that such thinking can actually cause sickness. If not, just use what you can accept from what you are reading. Remember that nobody gets into trouble by trying to correct distortions of logic when some sickness or other trouble impends.

By applying the technique to sickness, you may become one of those persons who has already produced a seemingly spontaneous recovery of what is thought to be an incurable disease.

Chapter 3

Formula for Preventing Trouble

SICKNESS IS obviously a sign that something has already gone wrong, and once sickness has come into being, it constitutes a problem to be solved. That is the old business of locking the barn door after the horse has been stolen. This book explains why people are not intelligent to let themselves become sick.

With the information already provided, people are intelligent to prevent sickness.

Of course, a person who is sick usually does not think that he had anything to do with causing the sickness. It could be expected that if he had known how he was causing the sickness, he would not have caused it. Very few people want to be sick, and after getting sick, the lack of information keeps them from knowing how they could have caused it.

All that changes when a person understands about distortions of logic.

By correcting distortions he can make changes in his thinking that eliminate the causes of many of his sicknesses. If he is sick as a result of something he did or failed to do, correcting distortions enables him to change what he does or doesn't do.

If he refuses to admit his responsibility, he is in a position of standing in his own light. So long as he obscures from himself the cause of his sickness, he cannot do anything to get rid of the cause. In that event he must depend on what might be done medically to counteract the cause.

The same is true of every other kind of trouble that is caused by the person who has the trouble. So long as he fails or refuses to consider the possibility that he caused the trouble himself, he must go on suffering from the trouble unless he can successfully counteract it in some way.

The feeling that trouble can properly be counteracted is responsible for a large amount of trouble that could be prevented, and the feeling that trouble is not preventable in many areas of life supports the proliferation of present-day adversity.

A person who knows that his life on the fast track is bad for his health may try to close his eyes to the connections between his sicknesses and his way of life. He may keep himself fortified with uppers and downers and antacids. He may believe that if he is smart, he can ward off the evil effects of his particular lifestyle.

If he used the same ingenuity correcting distortions, he would soon become rational about his way of life.

He would not have to deprive himself of it as he may if he continues and is told by his doctor that he must desist to survive. By correcting his distortions, he creates a situation in which his lifestyle strikes him as being illogical and wrong. Then he changes it.

There is another way in which the feeling that trouble can be counteracted contributes to continued trouble, and it is fundamental.

When a person is tempted to take illogical, wrong action, he always expects to gain something. Instinctively he tends to balance what he thinks he will gain against what he thinks he might lose. When he feels he can successfully counteract the losses, he assumes he is free to proceed.

By acting on that assumption, he makes a serious mistake.

One difficulty is that he cannot fully comprehend the losses. He detects only those that are obvious, and he fails to allow for the hidden losses that will presently result from that wrong thinking.

He has his mind on gratifying the urges based on his motives.

The process is illustrated by applying the foregoing reasoning to the way by which a person becomes a compulsive drinker.

Presumably such a person has heard about the dangers of excessive drinking, but he assumes he will be able to avoid them. He has his mind on the feeling of warm comfort that pervades his system when his blood has absorbed enough alcohol. He has his mind on his desired relief from tensions and on the feeling of buoyancy that he expects will repay him for drinking.

Those reasons seem logical to him.

If he could really get what he wants from drinking alcohol without the risk of paying too much for what he gets, compulsive drinking might not be considered too high a price to pay, but he doesn't think that out. He has his mind on his wants and how he can counteract the penalties he must pay for acting on those wants.

He may count the cost in money and decide he is willing to pay it. He may refuse to look beyond the cost of the next drink and thus refuse to consider the cost of a whole evening of drinks. He is not likely to consider the possibility that his earnings will be jeopardized if he shows up drunk on the job.

After he finishes counting the cost he is willing to pay, he tends to ignore the remainder.

He could consider the possibility that his drinking may destroy his employer's confidence in him, as is the case with many compulsive drinkers. So he may try to counteract that danger, not by moderating his drinking but by taking pains to hide it from his employer.

And so it goes.

The one thing that ordinarily is not done by a person engaged in the process of becoming a compulsive drinker is to face the facts of his growing compulsion. He hides those facts from himself by installing distortions as he goes along. Under that circumstance, he loses his ability to face his wrong thinking except by the indirect methods that are described in this book.

That is the real penalty of an assumption that trouble can be counteracted. It is a hidden penalty that everybody pays as a result of the emotional thinking by which he installs his distortions of logic.

From the foregoing it is clear that distortions are not always installed in a burst of obvious emotion. They may be installed in a burst of subtle emotion that may or may not contain anger. It may be a burst of lust or greed or pride or of any emotion that has the effect of stimulating illogical thinking and wrong action while reducing intelligence.

There are many such emotions that are not normally detected.

Everybody has experienced many emotions that have led him to install distortions. Because of those distortions, he naturally thinks that whatever kind of trouble he gets into is not his fault, but everybody needs to discover the error of that thought.

II

PERHAPS FEW persons are able, at this point, to accept the possibility that they cause all their own trouble. But every reader can recognize that many persons have trouble of their own causing that they blame on factors outside themselves.

That observation suggests a plan of action.

When some trouble arises, a person should pause and reflect. He should remember what has been said in these pages and consider the possibility that somehow the trouble resulted from illogical action on his part.

He should seek command phrases that could cause the trouble, and continue until he has found enough command phrases to give him some justification for assuming that he may have made the necessary corrections. Then he can see what develops.

He may discover that his thinking and behavior change enough to enable him to see that he did cause the trouble himself. At the same time, he probably would be in the position also of having stopped the trouble. After he has done that often enough, he may be willing to make revisions in the amount of trouble he feels he has caused himself.

Nobody has to force himself on that point.

Perhaps you will feel afraid to rely fully on the correction of distortions to protect you from trouble. If so, don't rely on it fully, but use any other measures you consider appropriate.

Consider an example in relation to health.

Suppose you have pernicious anemia. If so, perhaps you have been taking daily injections of liver extract for years to keep yourself alive. Continue whatever treatment your doctor recommends, but also correct distortions.

If your physical condition is caused by distortions, correcting them would change it. When that happens, let your doctor decide what to do about it.

You may at first suppose that the foregoing illustration is rather farfetched, but it has been included for a specific reason. The reason is not that many seemingly farfetched changes have resulted from correcting distortions, although they have, it is that anybody can use the technique of correcting distortions without abandoning any other procedure in which he has confidence.

His experience presently tells him what he can accomplish by use of the command phrase technique. Often a person fails to accomplish something beneficial because he fails to try. He should know that if the result is important, so will be the loss.

III

AFTER A person has corrected enough distortions so that he has gained real facility in bringing up command phrases, he learns that many kinds of trouble are his fault that he never suspected he caused.

Some of those troubles may not be entirely his fault.

In many situations he may be aware that someone else is responsible for part of a trouble as is likely to be true in cases of conflict, but he realizes that his part of the trouble is his fault.

From that observation, he learns about a principle of behavior.

The principle is that each person's part of every trouble is his own fault. Accepting it is easy for the persons who already know it, but for various reasons, accepting it is difficult for other persons.

The reader is not asked to accept it until he understands it.

All he is asked to do is to realize the obvious truth that people often fail to recognize when trouble is their own fault and to consider the possibility that some specific trouble is of his own making, even though at first it does not seem so.

There is real benefit in taking that attitude.

One benefit is that the foregoing attitude enables a person to stop trouble he would not be able to stop unless he does take that attitude. Therefore, failure to take that attitude limits what he can do for himself by correcting distortions.

Whenever distortions are corrected, many changes occur. Thinking, conversation and conduct on the subjects of the distortions change at once in accord with the corrections.

Those changes may or may not be evident to the individual.

Formula for Preventing Trouble

Since he has no consciousness of being illogical when he makes a change from illogical to logical thinking, he does not suddenly become conscious of being logical. He may have to look closely to detect the difference, but if he has suffered some serious problem solved by the corrections, he may see a very dramatic change.

Consider a few examples of such changes.

When a person who has corrected distortions on the appropriate subjects suddenly loses his craving for tobacco or alcohol or suddenly stops his long-standing habit of overeating and starts taking off the excess weight he could not previously lose, he is reasonable to suppose that he has successfully made those corrections.

The same is true in relation to many other problems.

Success in making corrections is to be judged by the changes that result. Not all those changes can be noticed, but that hardly matters. No harm can be done by exposing illogical thinking. After the wrong thinking has been exposed, the changes occur even if they are not sought or noticed.

A person could hardly miss such changes as cessation of smoking or drinking or overeating, but many changes he will know nothing about.

A command phrase he happens to locate in relation to overeating may also have influence in various other departments of his life. Suppose that the phrase is "I have to do everything I want to do." In that case the command phrase may contribute to compulsive smoking and drinking and also to cheating at cards or yelling at the children.

No effort need be made to analyze the results of any particular correction. Results are not gained by analyses but by exposing the appropriate command phrases and detecting their illogic.

Once a command phrase has been detected and its influence destroyed, a person should give it no more attention than he would give yesterday's garbage; he would just throw it out.

In case you are interested in stopping some particular kind of trouble, you are sensible to notice whether the trouble disappears or not. If it does, you have accomplished your purpose. If it doesn't, keep on trying. Persist at reasonable intervals until you succeed.

In some cases you may have to use technique over a period of time.

Apparently there is a natural sequence in which distortions are corrected. If a person tries to violate that sequence too seriously, he may not get the desired result until a later time.

When he succeeds in correcting a distortion, no matter what result he gets, two kinds of changes occur. First, he solves the problem that was caused by the distortion, provided the problem has not already caused irrevocable damage. Second, he prevents the problem from recurring.

The process for doing it is extremely simple. It is analogous to what happens when an individual makes some entirely objective change in a situation that has been causing trouble.

Suppose you have a loose carpet in a hallway outside your living room. If so, unwary visitors might trip. Suppose you decide that before you entertain some evening, you will remove the carpet and not replace it. If so, you solve the problem of whether any of your guests will trip over that carpet.

You can thus solve it for all time.

IV

THE LOGICAL way to solve a problem caused by illogical thinking is to correct the distortions of logic responsible for the illogical thinking, and that is also the logical way to prevent trouble.

Much of everybody's persistent trouble could thus be prevented.

As long as distortions persist, they continue causing whatever trouble their command phrases suggest. A person who knows nothing about distortions of logic is helpless to take basic preventive action.

But not a person who has that knowledge.

Ordinarily he does not correct distortions as a means of preventing trouble. He corrects them as a means of solving problems, but he has ways of using his knowledge of distortions also to prevent trouble in ways that are surprisingly effective.

V

THERE ARE two general ways a person uses knowledge of distortions to prevent trouble. The first way is that he notices when other persons are illogical because they are thinking through their distortions. The second way is to become sensitive enough that he can make the same observation in himself and thus avoid illogical conversation or behavior.

Those two ways will be dealt with in sequence.

Starting with illogical behavior in other persons serves the purpose best, because illogical behavior is easier to observe in others than in the person who is doing the observing.

People are not very skilled at catching their own examples of illogic. On the other hand, they are likely to be extremely sensitive to examples in other persons, particularly when their own interests are somehow involved in a way that might prove costly.

Initially the ability to detect illogical behavior is somewhat unreliable.

Nearly everybody supposes he can easily see illogical behavior in others, but what he does not realize, at first, is that he views the behavior of others through his own distortions.

Sometimes the illogic he observes in others is as much his own illogic as anybody's. Sometimes it is more.

The following example makes the point:

Suppose a person hears someone arguing heatedly over the faults of some special brand of cigarettes and considers those arguments to be illogical because he personally enjoys the brand being criticized. Then suppose he later destroys the distortions that cause him to smoke. In that case he would consider illogical various of the arguments he once used to justify his enjoyment of the brand criticized.

To that example can be hitched a basic statement regarding how the knowledge of distortions can be used to prevent trouble.

When you hear someone arguing heatedly about anything, you can be sure he is thinking through distortions. Only illogical thinking could explain his loss of emotional composure. In addition, only illogical, wrong thinking is done by a person who has lost his emotional composure.

Therefore, there are two reasons for being wary of him.

The advantage of a display of emotion is that it calls attention to the illogic of the person who is emotional. But people have acquired the ability to conceal their emotions, and that is a deceptive state of affairs.

The person who appears outwardly calm may be a seething inferno of emotions inside. He may control their outward display, but only because he has distortions demanding that he control them.

Then there is the person who is unreasonable.

The person who is unreasonable is not necessarily a person who is stupid and unintelligent. He is a person who has distortions that in one way or another cause him to be unreasonable. So long as he continues thinking through those distortions, he remains unreasonable.

Here are typical command phrases that may be involved:

"I'll never give in, no matter who opposes me." "Nobody can make me take a back seat in a discussion." "I'll get my way if it's the last thing I do." "When I make up my mind, I won't change it." "I'll never admit a mistake."

When a person is actuated by those distortions, arguing with him is pointless. Unless you can correct the distortions, you are wise to await more favorable conditions.

How will you know when they exist?

When he becomes reasonable in ways he was formerly unreasonable, and that can easily happen because many distortions get used only part of the time.

Consider the command phrase "I'll never give in, no matter who opposes me." Obviously that phrase will have greatest effect when someone is opposing him, especially if the person seems important. On the other hand, consider the phrase "Nobody can make me take a back seat in a discussion." That phrase relates only to a discussion. If someone could get his thinking across in a way other than a discussion, the distortion would not get restimulated.

The more you know about a person's distortions, the more easily you can deal with him.

Most people have already learned by experience that each person has his own special peculiarities. For example, many a wife has learned that she is unwise to expect her husband to be happy and conversational at the breakfast table. So she just moves over and makes room for his peculiarities, or else she gives him strong enough incentive to go against his inclinations and act the way he doesn't feel.

If she understands distortions, she knows exactly what she is dealing with and can allow for it sensibly. With enough understanding and cooperation from her husband, she can get his help in correcting the distortions.

Afterward he can behave rationally at breakfast.

That illustrates what can be done to avoid trouble with other persons by understanding how distortions control behavior, but a great deal more is accomplished by correcting illogical conversation and behavior in yourself.

Consider the wife of the husband just discussed. She may

easily blame her husband for his antisocial tendencies at breakfast because she doesn't understand them. As a result she may have contradictory trouble of her own.

Suppose she has distortions installed in early life while she sat at breakfast and listened to arguments between her parents over whether breakfast was a place to read the paper or a place to discuss the coming events of the day.

A child can easily become emotional over parental conflicts.

Perhaps in a moment of emotional thinking, she formed the thought "If I ever have a husband who tries to ignore me at breakfast, I'll make his life so miserable he'll wish he'd never married anybody—especially me."

In that case there will be trouble.

Assuming that the husband and wife know nothing about distortions and the trouble they cause, their whole married life could be thrown off balance by just a few command phrases that invite conflict in various ways. All such conflict would be minimized and even ended by applying the knowledge of distortions.

Either the husband or wife could make progress alone.

When a person thinks through distortions, he always experiences a certain amount of negative emotion. It may be an emotion he has difficulty recognizing, or it may be such an obvious emotion he cannot miss it.

His emotion is a tip-off so that when he is emotional, he can be sure that whatever he is getting ready to say or do will be tinged with the irrational influence of distortions.

If he is wise, he would not say or do anything at that moment.

If people understood distortions and applied that knowledge as just recommended, it would prevent a large number of persons from doing a large amount of the talking they have customarily done in the past. At first they might feel somewhat restricted, but if they kept quiet, they would learn that

Formula for Preventing Trouble

there is no loss.

If you were to add up all the conversations you have heard that you could wisely get along without, the total would be impressive.

Much of that conversation is eliminated as the simple result of understanding how distortions control thinking and conversation. The logical time to remember that is when someone's distortions are getting used, and it makes little difference in that respect whether the distortions are yours or his.

If you talk when you feel emotional, you are sure to talk through your distortions whether or not someone else is talking through his. When you see that the other person is emotional, you can be sure that he is talking through his distortions. If you want to compound confusion, just try putting all your emotions into words.

On the other hand by remaining silent, you may restore order.

Presently you may think of something to say that you are sure will do no harm. If you feel completely unemotional about it, you are likely to cause no trouble by trying it out. After enough experiments of that sort, you find yourself able to deal with situations that had formerly brought frustration.

At first you may feel that imposing such restrictions on yourself is a bit unfair. You may feel that other people should do the changing, not you. But the fact is that virtually never can you get others to change as you think they should.

Meanwhile you have to get along with them.

By making the recommended change all you lose is trouble. If you feel rebellious over the change, pause to reflect on the implications of rebellion. Remember that rebellion provides an emotional situation in which distortions are installed.

A person is well-advised to apply that information to every situation he faces. ***By learning never to react in rebellion*** *of any sort, no matter what the provocation, he also is able to avoid arguments and troublesome relationships.*

As a by-product, he gains something important.

A person thinks through his distortions most vigorously when he is emotional. Therefore, a person who habitually avoids emotion is less likely to express his distortions in conversation and behavior than a person who is often emotional.

The way to reduce emotion is to avoid rebelling against whatever is happening. The situations most likely to arouse rebellion need a rational response to handle them.

At first avoiding emotion is difficult, but with experience, it becomes instinctive for the person who understands distortions of logic and the trouble they cause. Why? Because he is able to trace out the sequences of cause and effect clearly enough to know what trouble he invites by his rebellion.

After that he has less difficulty controlling himself.

Chapter 4

Carefully Inspect Your Behavior

WHILE CONTROLLING recognizable outbursts of rebellion lets a person prevent much trouble, that is not enough. The reason is that many kinds of rebellion at first are unrecognizable.

What is rebellion?

In the broad sense, rebellion is unwillingness to accept life as it is and as it must be accepted if the individual is to avoid problems and trouble. It is unwillingness to face reality. It is unwillingness to be guided strictly by what the individual knows is right.

That definition establishes why it is that not all rebellion shows itself in emotional outbursts.

A person who loses his temper because he cannot get his way is displaying rebellion, but in the broad sense, so does a person who tries to cheat in a game or in a financial transaction.

He is unwilling to accept life as it unfolds.

Of course, he is free to improve his condition by taking any kind of action he knows is right. But if he tries to improve his condition by taking any kind of action he knows is wrong, he is engaged in an act of rebellion. He is not accepting life honestly and realistically.

By his rejection he damages his moral code.

All distortions of logic involve damage to a person's moral codes on the unconscious level, and that is where the moral codes exist. Often he may conversationally express a moral code that his daily behavior habitually contradicts. His trouble is that while he consciously expresses one kind of thinking, his unconscious distortions cause him to express a different behavior. ***Therefore, his behavior is a better indication of his true moral code than his conversation.***

His behavior is controlled by his distortions to an extent that may seem unbelievable by a person who has not carefully investigated the facts.

The truth is that the average person spends his life unknowingly trying to gratify his distortions. By the time he is an adult, he has little remaining freedom of action. From one year's end to the next, he seldom or never does anything, directly or indirectly, not called for by the command phrases of his distortions.

Each distortion is really a fixed deviation from what he had once regarded as a correct interpretation of morality. He installed the distortion by departing from what he considered right. In doing the thinking by which he installed the distortion, he rationalized the behavior he had previously considered wrong.

By adjusting his thinking, he made it seem right.

He changed his moral code on the unconscious level by deciding on the conscious level to take some action that would have the effect of violating his conscious moral code.

That is how people damage their morals.

The process of progressive deviation is extremely subtle. A person never makes a gigantic deviation in a single step. He makes a series of minor deviations and mentally blinds himself to each deviation by installing it in a hidden distortion. Therefore, his next deviation seems just about as trivial as the previous deviation.

By that sort of thinking, small deviations become large.

A person who prides himself on his refusal to do anything that seems really wrong to him can install trivial distortions in a steady but always forgotten stream; thus unwittingly he

Carefully Inspect Your Behavior

can reduce himself to such levels of depravity that his behavior is shocking.

Until he learns about distortions, he cannot know that he has done it.

Every person who can dispassionately analyze what has just been explained is thereby given possession of extremely important and valuable information. He no longer needs to wonder why people sometimes do outrageous things.

Suddenly he can understand what causes the acts of astonishing bestiality for which some members of the human race get publicity. He can understand, for example, how a person given the advantages of a good early home life could become a sex maniac by entering first one and then another situation in which he made small sex deviations that he acted on and incorporated into his network of distortions.

More important, he can understand why the persons he knows all have higher opinions of their behavior than the facts warrant.

Most important, he can understand that his own predicament urgently needs attention because he himself is much further from the ideal path of life than he has supposed.

That knowledge lets him do something to improve matters.

II

IN ADDITION to correcting distortions and thus ridding himself of their blighting effects on his life, an informed person does his best to stop, for all time, the process of installing more distortions.

He decides he should monitor his behavior.

One of the easiest ways for a person to get started is to make himself highly sensitive to his moments of rebellion. **The reason is that he never installs distortions except when he tries to reject the unfolding events of life and substitute some**

new element of his own devising.

Over a period of time, he learns to detect rebellion that formerly he would not have called rebellion.

Not only does he prevent installation of distortions by that procedure, but he also tends to give less expression to the distortions he has already installed. He recognizes that his emotional thinking reflects the fact that distortions are getting used.

The greater the emotion, the more distortions get restimulated.

Of course that is to be expected. Everybody has made the observation that a person who is highly emotional, as when suffering a violent outburst of temper, becomes highly illogical and behaves irrationally.

When strong emotion develops, something about the chemistry of the body apparently acts to cause connections between brain cells constituting the closed mental circuits of distortions to become better conductors. The distortions that go into restimulation at such times are the ones installed under the same general kinds of emotion as are getting expressed.

A person who feels the emotion characteristic of larceny tends to think through distortions causing him to commit thefts. A person who has the emotion of unreasoning fear in relation to germs tends to think through distortions making him take extreme precautions to avoid exposure to germs.

Similar examples could be cited in every area of life.

Occasionally a person is caught in such a violent outburst of many kinds of emotion that his distortions simultaneously try to drive him in several contradictory directions.

The following example illustrates what happens:

Suppose a person is caught in some embarrassing wrong act and is publicly shamed in front of a group of persons who know him well and whose good opinions he values. He would display many kinds of discomfort.

He might repeatedly blush and then turn pale because of the promptings of his command phrases. He might try to stand and fight and then, in turn, try to run and hide with the result that he would tremble violently. He might try to speak up to defend himself and also remain silent with the result that his lips would move but no words would be spoken.

His violent emotional reaction to his predicament would cause so many promptings from distortions that he could not act on more than a small proportion of them. Obviously he could not behave logically and rationally.

Some persons may remember having been in a predicament similar to the extreme case just cited, but in a lesser sense, everybody is in somewhat that predicament all the time.

Because of distortions, he is constantly pushed in a variety of contradictory directions with the result that his behavior subtly deviates from paths of logic without his realization. Because his distortions have usurped his volition, he cannot control his behavior directly. Because he considers himself logical when he does whatever his distortions prompt him to do, he is helpless in their grip.

Of course, he changes matters by correcting distortions.

But each person has so many distortions that he needs much time to bring his behavior under control if he tries to do it by efforts that are casual and spasmodic.

Therefore, he needs a method that is quick.

III

IN ADDITION to making scrupulous efforts to avoid rebellious reactions, he can also try to avoid making wrong decisions. At first that statement seems to have a moral flavor, and it may seem like the statement of a reformer.

Anybody who chooses to do so can leave moral considerations out of his thinking and be guided by practical considerations only. It so happens that a decision that is wrong in a practical sense is also morally wrong, although some persons may dispute that statement.

There is a reason why a person is not reached on a moral plane. It is that he has desensitized his conscience on exactly those points on which he cannot agree that morality and practicality are identical. That is one of the results of installing distortions.

Consider the following example:

Suppose a person was brought up to believe that stealing is wrong. Then he gets a job. He sees other workers taking home occasional items of company property, but he refrains because of his early training. Then one day he needs a paper clip. He considers the item so small that the act of taking it does not really seem at all like stealing. So he takes the paper clip.

Presently he advances to postage stamps. Later still he is taking the items he formerly criticized his fellow workers for taking. In that manner he lowers his moral code in imperceptible stages.

On each point he embodied the alteration in his distortions so that it became undetectable to him. In the process he has desensitized his conscience on each of those points.

If anyone has the audacity to tell him he is a thief, he becomes so emotional and illogical he is impossible to deal with. Yet he is a thief. He made himself a thief over a period of time by making one deviation after another from what he once considered right, and he cannot be approached on a moral plane.

He is touchy on the subject of morality. He cannot understand the morality he has blanked out until he has restored it; then he does not need to have it explained.

Because of those considerations, it would seem that the best comprehensive approach is one that leaves out morality and instead is based on practical considerations.

With that as a preliminary, we should put attention on a little known law of behavior.

Fundamental to life is the law of absolute right. It states: Right action gets right results, whereas wrong action gets wrong results. Therefore, no person can do what he considers wrong without first rationalizing what he had formerly considered wrong so that it seems right.

The conscious part of the process has long been understood, but what has not been understood is the unconscious part. That is the dangerous part. Nobody has any very strong reason to fear what he can understand and control, because he can protect himself from it. By contrast everybody has strong reason to fear the adverse effect of changes in his own thinking from right to wrong that are concealed from him and exert a compulsive influence in changing his behavior.

A fact that, at first, surprises people is that the law of absolute right needs no definitions of absolute right.

If you try to tell someone about absolute right, the chances are that he will evade your meanings. When you tell him that two plus two always equals four, he may tell you that Einstein was able to prove that sometimes two plus two doesn't equal four. If you tell him a man should have only one wife, he may tell you about certain countries where more than one wife is legal.

Those evasions serve only to cloud the real issue.

A person who lives by the law of absolute right is a person who is guided quite strictly by his own definitions of right and wrong, whatever they are. When he adds two and two and gets four, he does not try to say he got some number other than four. When he proposes marriage to someone, he does not tell her he is not already married if he is.

In every situation of life, he does what he considers to be right.

Whether a person likes it or not, he is bound by what he considers right. He may have altered what he considers right by installing distortions of logic over the period of his life, but for better or worse, he is bound by the definitions he has formed.

Of course, everybody's definitions are wrong in many ways.

When a person stops making compromises with what he considers right, he stops installing distortions. There is another kind of deviation from right that he can also bring under control quite directly.

One kind of distortion tells a person that the wrong action suggested by the command phrase of the distortion is not wrong but right. Another kind tells a person that even though the action suggested by the distortion is wrong, the action is justified. Both kinds have the effect of causing him to take any action under a delusion that he is right.

The following are examples of both kinds:

"You are always right to take action that will increase security for the persons whose welfare is in your hands." "Even though lying is not exactly right, there are some occasions when it is really right to misrepresent a few facts to get an important result."

A person with those command phrases will act in accord with them every time he faces a situation calling for such action with strong enough emotional force. While doing so, he may have no sense of being wrong—unless he understands the law of absolute right.

In that case he carefully tries as hard as he can to avoid any action that he has any reason to consider wrong.

That attitude enables him to catch his examples of wrong behavior that represent action he knows violates some really valid moral principle. It helps him to correct distortions that have the effect of justifying behavior he considers wrong, because he knows that wrong action cannot be justified.

As fast as those distortions go into restimulation because of events of life, they tend to call themselves to his attention.

He releases them simply by refusing to act on them, without even taking time to bring up and analyze their command phrases. He experiences no sense of loss.

The only reason a person does what he considers wrong is that he expects to gain more than he loses. If he understands distortions and the problems and trouble they cause, he is well aware that no wrong action could possibly bring any gain large enough to compensate for the loss.

For that reason, he loses his incentive to disregard the principle of absolute right: Think, say and do what is right. Refuse to think, say and do what is wrong.

Presently he is able to accomplish more than the reversals of thinking resulting from not taking action he knows is wrong by his own standards. He becomes aware that in addition to his own private wavering standards there are absolute standards in every area of life.

In the beginning there is no use trying to tell him that.

Each person is so accustomed to justifying his own deviations from right action that he feels an unconscious and perhaps even conscious vested interest in preserving the belief that there are no absolute and reliable standards by which to live.

Accepting that belief puts a ceiling on his thinking.

After a person has accepted the concept of distortions and has decided to apply it in his life to restore his logic and intelligence, he acquires a strong interest in finding absolute standards so that he can speed his progress.

Certain of those standards are not difficult to find, though he is unwise to start by trying to be comprehensive. Distortions have a sufficiently deceptive effect that a person succeeds best by not trying to make an initial comprehensive approach.

For example, he may have distortions telling him that he should constantly seek to prove his intelligence to everybody as a means of guaranteeing his security. In that case he will be totally insensitive to any suggestion that a person is wrong to try to prove his intelligence, although every person who has advanced to the necessary stage of understanding knows that it is irrational for anybody to try to prove his intelligence.

Few persons are at first willing to accept that, and no effort will be made to get anybody to accept it.

Getting people to accept the concept that trying to prove intelligence is wrong in this distorted society is usually impossible, except for the persons who understand about distortions and how they influence thinking. Presumably it will remain impossible until that number of persons increases.

We live in a world in which people seem to feel called on to prove their intelligence to the people around them much of the time.

Even though that effort causes frustration, it continues.

The reason it is frustrating is explained by the fact that no one can prove his intelligence to a person who at the same time is intent on proving his own intelligence. And that is what usually confronts the person who makes any such effort. He is trying to convince someone who just doesn't care and, therefore, refuses to give the matter his serious attention except to contradict it.

The reason the effort to prove intelligence continues is that the person who makes the effort is always driven by distortions he doesn't suspect afflict him. If he would stop to consider the matter, he would realize that he gains nothing of value by inducing people to admit his intelligence; therefore, the effort is a waste of time and it gets wrong results.

Perhaps the foregoing explanation may enable the earnest seeker after truth to understand why trying to prove intelligence is wrong, but that is not why the explanation was included.

A person who accepts the explanation is usually a person who needs no explanation because he has made the appropriate corrections. Or he may be a person who has distortions telling him to be modest and retiring. In any case he tends to be guided and controlled, without his realization, by whatever distortions happen to apply, rather than by any explanation contradicting them.

The explanation was included to show, if possible, the difficulty of trying to talk in terms of the fine distinctions between right and wrong. To a person who does not need the explanation, it is superfluous. To a person who does need the explanation, it is quite incomprehensible and, therefore, does not change his thinking.

Despite the fact that the fine distinctions between right and wrong are difficult to discuss, there are broad definitions that are obvious even to a person who sometimes may stoutly declare that there are no reliable distinctions.

For example, lying is wrong by definition.

That is enough for a person who understands distortions of logic. Such a person realizes that installing every distortion really involves a process by which the individual successfully lies to himself and thus gives himself a permanent delusion that he accepts in lieu of reality. Therefore, he refuses to lie.

In the past many persons, at first, rejected that.

They were persons who had numerous distortions telling them in various ways that certain kinds of lying are not really wrong but right. They talked of little white lies told for noble purposes. They were, of course, deluded.

There is no such thing as a little white lie.

Perhaps the best definition is that a little white lie is the kind of lie that is told by the person who offers the definition. **Actually every little white lie has a big black heart.**

IV

EVEN THAT explanation does not change the thinking of a person who insists on justifying lying. He has motives to contradict the truth and thinks he is not obligated to accept truth just because it is true. He thinks he is free to accept or reject truth according to what helps or hinders his efforts to satisfy his personal motives.

That is a common mistake.

If there were no distortions of logic, perhaps that would not be a mistake. In that case any person could freely make whatever compromises with truth happened to suit his motives. He could carefully analyze the consequences and decide whether, in light of those consequences, he should or should not act.

That is precisely the pattern of behavior that characterizes people's conduct.

When a person knows nothing about distortions, he is not restricted by any realization that wrong action involves serious hidden penalties brought on by attempted violations of the law of absolute right.

Therefore, people have a false sense of freedom.

With knowledge of that law and of distortions of logic, a person loses that false sense of freedom. *He may not be willing to become right just for the sake of being right, but he is willing to become right when he knows that being wrong is the process of inviting problems and trouble, regardless of what he supposes he gains by being wrong.*

It must be admitted that he does often seem to gain.

The quickest way to obtain a large sum of money may be to steal it, and the person who steals it successfully is certainly in a position to spend it. By stealing he gains money he did not have. Customarily the person who contemplates stealing considers whether he might be caught and punished and whether the amount of money to be stolen is large enough to justify the risks.

He does not consider what he will lose by taking wrong action and installing distortions of logic.

The really serious result of successful stealing is found in the distortions a person installs by the thinking that justi-

Carefully Inspect Your Behavior 73

fies the stealing. That result is a loss of intelligence and the replacement of right faculties with distortions. The victim never connects the cause with its effect until he understands distortions and how they are formed.

After he understands those factors, he knows that he pays for every wrong thought and act by the loss of some of his intelligence. If he has enough intelligence left, he knows that nobody has any intelligence to spare. Therefore, he concentrates on getting back all his lost intelligence as fast as he can.

That is something he can do by using the command phrase technique to correct distortions.

In addition to his enthusiasm to correct them, he develops an equal enthusiasm to prevent new distortions from forming. He wants to learn as much as he can about the distinctions between right and wrong so that he can live in accord with what is right.

He can always find a place to begin.

Even the person who, at first, cannot accept the idea that all lying is wrong can find some absolute definition of wrong action that he is able to accept.

For example, he may agree that someone who deliberately murders an infant because he likes to watch the spurting of blood is a person who is taking wrong action. He may admit that burning down schools and churches is wrong action and that purposely driving an automobile through a crowd of pedestrians is also wrong action.

If he can't do better, let him start there.

Of course, he may say that such wrongs are so obvious that nobody could miss them. That is the point. Every wrong is so obvious nobody could miss it unless he has distortions that impair his intelligence.

Until a person thinks he has corrected all his distortions, he should be cautious.

One of the ways he can help himself to be cautious is to arrive at reliable definitions of right and wrong and regard them as absolute. Because society has reached no general agreement regarding those definitions, he finds that he must arrive at them himself.

Having established a definition, the person who desires to regain his intelligence should live by that definition regardless of the seeming cost.

Actually he discovers there is no cost.

A person really cannot get into trouble by being right. He gets into trouble by being wrong. He may gain something by being wrong, but he always pays more for it than it is worth, and he may lose something by being right, but he gains something far more precious.

There is a reason why people have not learned that.

They are not trying to be right. Instead, they are trying to satisfy their motives, and in that effort, they make many wrong choices.

Actually they do not make choices that are consciously devoted to considerations of right and wrong. Little of their thinking is done on that basis. People make their choices on the basis of what has the most value in helping them to advance and satisfy their personal motives. Instead of trying to be right, they try to do, be, have, get, and become whatever they want and try to avoid what they want to avoid. Seldom do considerations of right and wrong influence their thinking unless they sense a threat to their motives.

All that kind of thinking changes for the person who gains understanding of distortions and the problems and trouble they cause.

Additionally he gains the missing ingredient of information that tells him why people have been in trouble so long. He learns that he is intelligent to base his choices on the distinctions between right and wrong. He also learns that when he cannot satisfy a motive without choosing wrong, he is wise to sacrifice the motive.

At first a person may be afraid to live that way.

His fear is empty, but it seems real nevertheless. If he proceeds in spite of his fear, he gradually discovers for himself that the fear is empty, and he is not required to take anyone's word for it.

In the process of making his change of motivation, he need take no chances.

He is required to do what he considers logical even if he believes it is wrong. But when his logic tells him to do something he knows is wrong, he can pause and check his logic. Instead of trying to determine whether he can get away with the wrong action, he can think about how he can safely change it to right action.

Usually under that circumstance, he sees what to do at once.

After a few experiences of that sort, he learns to train himself carefully to be present minded. Instead of compulsively acting in an effort to satisfy his personal motives, he tries to pursue a present-minded effort always to think, say and do what is right.

That is the safe, fundamental principle for a successful life.

Chapter 5

Houseclean Your Emotional Life

TRYING TO think, say and do what is right stops many tendencies that have had the effect of disturbing a person's emotional life. As a natural result, he gives himself fewer reasons to feel guilty.

That is an important benefit, because the average person carries a great burden of guilt.

Modern thinking has tended to excuse him for it, and that is characteristic of people's unconscious efforts to protect their distortions. Telling a person that he should not feel guilty is only a way of helping him to bury his conscience more deeply.

He cannot square himself with his conscience by burying it.

When he feels guilty, he is guilty. When he stops feeling guilty, it is not necessarily because he has stopped being guilty. The matter is not that simple.

His feeling of guilt may result from having committed wrongs that he knows he committed and knows are wrong. It may result from having installed distortions telling him to feel guilty. Or it may result from having committed wrongs about which he has no conscious memory.

However, his unconscious mind never forgets because it retains the data.

If a person feels guilty for any of the three foregoing reasons, distortions are involved. If nothing else, he is guilty of having done the wrong and illogical thinking by which he installed the distortions.

If he corrects the distortions, he stops feeling guilty. Unless he corrects the distortions, he cannot get rid of the burden of guilt although, as indicated earlier, he may stop noticing it consciously.

What has happened in that case?

A person who stops feeling guilty without correcting the distortions causing him to feel guilty is a person who has installed one or more additional distortions that have the effect of destroying his ability to continue noticing his feelings of guilt.

He still has them though.

Despite the fact that he may no longer notice his guilty feelings, he has some other kind of emotional or perhaps physical trouble that replaces the feelings of guilt. That is not mere speculation. It is a fact that is evident to every person who understands distortions.

The following example defines the sequence of cause and effect:

A person has a motive to get something he wants for which he has insufficient funds. After a time, he falsifies financial records at his place of employment so that he can help himself to the needed funds. Then he tries as hard as he can to forget the whole performance. He installs numerous command phrases justifying and excusing his theft.

Presently he succeeds in consciously forgetting the incident.

Now and again he notices an odd feeling of guilt that he cannot explain. Increasingly it burdens him. Occasionally it angers him. In one of his angry moments, he does the rebellious thinking necessary to cause installation of more distortions necessary to destroy his ability to notice his feelings of guilt.

Here are possible command phrases:

"I have no reason to feel guilty." "I've never done anything any worse than what everybody else does." "Instead of feeling guilty, I should feel proud of my accomplishments."

Enough phrases of that sort can blanket the guilt completely.

After that has been done, it may appear as though the individual has released himself from his feelings of guilt, but such is not the case. He still has them. He has merely given himself an obligation to avoid recognizing them as such.

It causes an unconscious battle to go on inside among his emotions, and that battle never really ceases. He has given himself a set of unconscious emotions, causing him distress; then he gives himself another set of unconscious emotions to hold them in check. All he really accomplishes is to increase his total unconscious burden, although he has changed its form. He would have been better off to get rid of the burden by correcting the original distortions.

That is not a farfetched example.

Of course, it is unusual. A usual example would seem incomprehensible because of many persons' distortions. For that reason, the example must be one that does not afflict many persons because no reader who is afflicted by it could understand it. Merely reading about the example could ring so many unconscious bells that he might be rendered emotionally unable to continue reading.

Nevertheless the example is realistic.

Everybody knows that people do misappropriate funds by altering financial records. Everybody knows that people are able to blank out portions of their memories under some conditions. Everybody knows that people do try to deceive themselves in their moments of emotion.

Those are the elements of the example cited.

What a person may not realize is that he himself has installed many thousand distortions that have the effect of setting up all sorts of unconscious conflicts, tending to destroy his peace of mind. He cannot restore that peace of mind unless he gets rid of those conflicts. He cannot get rid of those conflicts unless he corrects the distortions by which they were created.

His usual efforts to remedy the situation fail.

The reason they usually fail is that often he tries to use objective means of counteracting something that is really subjective in nature.

Men of science have had difficulty grappling with that problem.

The reason for their difficulty is that science is generally limited to objective techniques, whereas a distortion of logic is not easily understood except by subjective analysis.

Science has tended to avoid subjective analyses.

Actually subjective thinking is fully as reliable as objective thinking, provided the person who does the thinking makes due allowance for distortions. They are what make subjective thinking unreliable. Resort to objective thinking enables the thinking person to check his accuracy by objective means.

It is for that reason that use of the principle of absolute right is able to restore logical thinking. Measuring behavior against an objective standard enables the individual to determine when he is wrong. That tells him his behavior is actuated by distortions, at least to the extent that he reasons from valid standards of right.

So long as a person lacks scientific experience in working with subjective principles, he needs objective principles from which to reason. After he gains experience with subjective principles, he can deal with the subjective nature of distortions.

Until he gains such experience, distortions are a closed book to him. He can read about distortions and fail to understand any of the information he needs to deal with them successfully.

Of course, some efforts to restore rationality may succeed

despite a lack of familiarity with distortions of logic.

When a person actually succeeds in facing a truth that has been hidden from him, no matter what his approach, he gets a correction. The reason he faces the truth may be that he is compelled to face it by some event of life.

Consider the following examples:

A person may delude himself into believing he can violate the law of gravity, but when he tries to do it, he gets bumped. Presently he gets his delusion corrected, or else he fails to survive one of those bumps.

A person may delude himself into believing he does not engage in a certain kind of wrong behavior considered offensive by others. When he is confronted with a piece of evidence that he cannot deny, even to himself, his delusion is shattered.

For instance, he may delude himself into believing he had no connection with the circulation of an ugly rumor, but when a therapist helps him to recapture blanked-out memories, he sees the connection if it is there.

Any procedure that has the effect of enabling the individual to see a piece of blanked-out truth restores logical thinking on the subject of that truth. Any problem or trouble caused by blanked-out truth that is supplanted by untruth remains a problem or trouble until the truth is exposed.

Exposing the truth restores normalcy.

Because truth is supplanted with untruth only by the process of installing distortions of logic, correcting distortions is the right way to restore the truth that was lost and to eliminate the untruth that replaced it. Any other method of dealing with the situation is beyond the reach of the person who has the distortions.

At first some persons suppose that there is a conflict between the process of correcting distortions and the process of admitting wrongs and transgressions to gain a spiritual benefit.

It is not the purpose of this book to deal with spiritual benefits.

The information contained here is intended to restore logical thinking where it has been lost. Nevertheless it is a fact that admitting wrongs and transgressions misses the real objective as far as restoration is concerned, because in the presence of distortions, their full admission is impossible—for a solid reason.

The individual cannot admit what he knows nothing about. He may know about his behavior, although probably some of that is forgotten. But it is certain that he does not know about his distortions. It is also certain that he does not know about the thinking that caused the installation of the distortions.

It is that thinking that is dangerous.

Until he regards that thinking as something in the nature of a wrong and a transgression, he has no motive to admit it. Actually admitting that it is in the nature of a wrong and a transgression is the precise performance that corrects the distortions.

Once the distortions are corrected, logic on the subject of the distortions is restored. Thereafter the individual can go as fast and as far as he likes in the direction of admitting his wrongs and transgressions to gain spiritual benefit.

II

EMOTIONAL BENEFIT he gains at once. Sometimes he feels a sensation of sudden release, especially when the distortion has the direct effect of causing emotional tension.

Consider the following command phrases of that sort:

"I feel tense all the time." "I'm always afraid of what is going to happen next." "I'm strung up like a violin." "I can't help being excited." "No matter what is going to happen, I

know it won't be good." "I just can't control my emotions."
Anybody can remember thinking such things.

Originally they were formulated under conditions that invited emotion, and because of the emotion, they became command phrases able to dominate and magnify every invitation to emotion of the same general kind.

A person who spends a few minutes each day running all such sentences through his mind is soon able to produce remarkable improvement in his habitual emotional state.

He need only recognize that the sentences are command phrases.

Getting rid of all of them cannot be accomplished in a single effort. The average person has great numbers of command phrases. Even if he disposes of them on one subject, he will still have emotional tension in other areas.

The reason for that tension is that every distortion is an unconscious-level pocket of emotional tension that remains until the distortion is corrected. A person who intends to rid himself of all emotional tension has a long road to travel.

At first consideration, traveling that road may seem hopeless, but it isn't.

In the beginning emotional tension may seem to result from various causes other than your own distortions. Wrong action on the part of other persons is especially suspect. When that happens, correct distortions on the subject of your reactions to other persons' actions, and you will find the state of your emotions undergoes a change. Sometimes emotional tension seems to result from your failure to perform various important tasks. If so, correct the distortions that interfere with your willingness or ability to perform those tasks.

If you keep up that sort of thinking, you will presently conclude that distortions are behind just about everything that goes wrong with a person. Go as far in that direction as you are able.

III

AS YOU continue to correct distortions, you will find you are housecleaning your entire emotional life. You won't enjoy all of the process, because facing disagreeable truth about yourself is sometimes necessary.

Nobody enjoys that prospect, but unless you face that disagreeable truth, you will continue to get into various kinds of trouble because of your distortions. On the other hand if you are willing to face it, you will bring to a halt one kind of trouble after another.

Presently you will realize that you have transformed your life and that many kinds of problems and trouble that you had long considered unavoidable no longer exist.

You can get that sort of result by searching out command phrases in an effort to eliminate problems and trouble. As you get rid of one kind, you will become able to recognize other kinds. Increasingly you will recognize situations in which you had been wrong, although you had thought you were right.

As fast as those situations come to light, deal with them.

Gradually you will increase the reliability of your standards of right and wrong and acquire definitions of wrong action that you would have vigorously denied before you understood distortions. You will make changes in your definitions of honesty that are incomprehensible by the average person.

Consider the following example:

The average person considers he is being intelligent to misrepresent the state of his health and his feelings. When he wants sympathy, he tells people how sick he feels. When he wants to make a good impression on his boss, he tells people in his boss's hearing how well he feels. Almost always when asked how he feels, he uses some stock answer that bears little relationship to the truth.

At first the foregoing paragraph may seem extreme and

somewhat like hairsplitting. So whether or not you think it is hairsplitting depends on your definition of hairsplitting.

In any case, truth is truth so long as it conforms with reality.

There is nothing indefinite about reality. Despite a lot of misguided thinking, truth that conforms with reality is right, and right is absolute.

The fact that a person who misrepresents his health does so unthinkingly is no excuse as far as distortions are concerned. Every person has an obligation to be cautious about his thinking. Otherwise he is in the position of a person who takes a chance by disregarding his behavior.

If he happens to be standing in front of an approaching automobile because he is not thinking about what he is doing, the fact that his being there was inadvertent does not save him from injury or possible death.

Anyone who thinks the foregoing example splits hairs will be more distressed by the next example.

Not only does the average person habitually misrepresent the state of his health, but he tries even harder to misrepresent the state of his emotions. He does that partly by not letting the true state of his emotions show in his facial expression. Millions of persons go about their daily affairs wearing smiles or frowns that do not belong on their faces but are worn for the purpose of creating a desired effect.

However that practice is defined, it is not honest.

A person who intends to houseclean his emotional life ultimately goes the whole way or else he gives up his intention. If he intends to go the whole way, the sooner he starts, the better.

With every change of thinking from wrong to right, he corrects distortions. With every correction of distortions, he improves his emotional life. Therefore, he has strong incentive to improve his standards of behavior in every possible way, at every opportunity, as rapidly as he reasonably can.

That is something he can do by facing every kind of truth, however disagreeable.

If he keeps that up long enough to get really substantial experience with the results of correcting distortions, he learns that for him there is no longer any such thing as a disagreeable truth.

He learns that the only thing really to fear is any refusal to face truth. He learns that truth directs his attention to reality and that truth confirmed by reality really does make him free.

IV

IN ADDITION to facing truth by locating command phrases and seeing their illogic and by seeking absolute standards of right thought and behavior, another procedure gets remarkable results.

At first, it seemingly goes against natural inclinations.

People are so constructed that they have an inherent wish to avoid admitting to themselves and others that they are wrong. That is what has caused people to fail throughout the centuries to recognize the nature of distortions and start getting them corrected.

In the beginning, the whole idea seems offensive.

The person who learns what correcting distortions can do for him knows he has more reason for feeling injured if someone tries to prevent him from correcting distortions than if someone tries to induce him to correct them.

The next procedure should be considered in that light.

The procedure relates to the private collection of disagreeable recollections everybody harbors in his unconscious mind.

One characteristic of those recollections is that they do not always remain in the unconscious mind. Instead, they try repeatedly to make their presence known by impinging on the consciousness of their possessor. Each time one rises into his consciousness, he winces and tries to push it back where it came from.

He may assume he is the only person who has such memories.

The reason for that is that nobody likes to discuss the collection of mental rubbish that he would like to dispose of but can't. So nobody learns just how much trouble of that kind infests the conscious and unconscious minds of people everywhere.

The total quantity is staggering.

For any specific person, it is large. The average person has no idea how large because he has no way of taking inventory. At any given time, he may be unable to remember a single example, but let him take attention away from the effort to remember, and presently one of them bobs up.

After a year of collecting examples, if he were to keep a record, he would be surprised by the total number.

There is a way to get rid of them.

Before considering that, give attention to an example that shows how they are dealt with by the average person.

Suppose you find a piece of rubbish on your desk. Presumably you would put it in the wastebasket. If you return to your desk a few hours later and find the same piece of rubbish on your desk, you would again put it in the wastebasket.

If you find that same piece of rubbish returning to your desk again and again, you will presently be justified in supposing that something is wrong with your rubbish-disposal system.

So it is with mental rubbish.

The fact that disagreeable memories return again and again to plague their possessor proves that he has not discovered how to get rid of them, and that is because the disagreeable memory absorbs all his attention. He is so intent on pushing the memory out of consciousness and forgetting it that he neglects to observe he does not have a suitable system for disposing of it.

Any effort to think about such a system causes him to keep on remembering the disagreeable memory that he wants above all else to forget. He does not even pause to reflect on the reason why his disagreeable memories keep recurring.

Of course, there is a reason. His unconscious mind is trying to get him to give the disagreeable memories proper attention.

Next time some disagreeable memory arises to make you wince inwardly, try to remember that. At first it may be difficult because habit tends to cause the same old reaction, but presently you can master the procedure that enables you to dispose of the disagreeable memory.

Next, the procedure is described.

Instead of pushing the disagreeable memory out of mind, pause and inspect it closely. Look for some special piece of disagreeable truth in it that you have been refusing to admit to yourself. Face that piece of truth in absolute honesty.

It will contain something uncomplimentary to you.

What your unconscious mind is trying to do is to get you to face that particular element of the disagreeable memory. Once you have faced it, the memory ceases to be disagreeable. It may even seem laughable.

It is not what a person knows about that causes his reluctance. It is what is hidden.

Bring out what is hidden and the reluctance vanishes. What must you bring out? Usually something that tells you how you were at fault in the situation to which the disagreeable memory relates.

Admit your fault to yourself.

You need not admit it to anyone else nor call the incident to anybody's attention. Until you honestly and frankly admit the fault to yourself, the disagreeable memory will continue to recur and plague you from time to time. If it recurs after you have admitted your wrongness, it will no longer be distressing.

How can you be sure that the attention you give a disagreeable memory really exposes the hidden truth?

First, you will see something in it you did not see previously. Perhaps you will discover additional details of the memory itself. Or perhaps you will see how you were wrong in ways you had thought you were right.

Second, you will feel a sudden sense of emotional relief as you realize the memory is no longer disagreeable.

In various instances you will be required to face more than one disagreeable element in such a memory before you get full release. If there are two or more pieces of disagreeable truth, you must face them all before you can dispose of the incident.

You can help yourself by trying to put the disagreeable truth into specific words.

The following sentences may come to mind:

"I was wrong when I said I didn't know." "Everybody present saw that I was dishonest, and that is what I haven't been able to admit to myself." "I certainly did make myself look stupid." "It's been just too much for me to admit to myself that I could have made that awful mistake."

Such conversation with yourself need not be disagreeable.

You will be telling those things only to yourself. When properly considered, they get you out of trouble and not into it. They provide a kind of emotional satisfaction that is difficult to describe and probably impossible to understand in advance. More important, they bring freedom.

An occasional disagreeable memory may arouse such strong fear that, at first, you are reluctant to use the foregoing procedure. No matter. Skip that one. Wait for a memory you think you can approach successfully and without excessive disturbance.

After you have disposed of a few memories of that sort, you will have enough experience to know what you are doing. Presently you will be willing to tackle any memory that arises.

You will be doing what your unconscious mind has been trying to get you to do all along.

When a person realizes the importance of getting rid of emotional rubbish, he feels eager to collect all the samples he can find so that he can apply the technique and be released from them.

Making any effort to find them is unnecessary.

Let them come to mind as they will. The unconscious mind will deliver them in sequence, always when you are in a position to do something about disposing of them.

Accept the natural sequence.

When one of your disagreeable memories does arise, you need not give it any more attention than has been your habit in the past. All that is necessary is that you give it the proper kind of attention described earlier in this chapter. You can learn to deal with its hidden message as fast or faster than you can push the disagreeable memory out of your conscious mind.

And if you do, you get rid of the disagreeable part.

Chapter 6

Improve Your Effects on People

ELIMINATING A disagreeable memory by the procedure described in the preceding chapter is, of course, a process of correcting one or more distortions.

In effect, that process uses memory of an incident and ignores command phrases. But if you carefully rummage around in your mind after using that procedure, you will be able to find the command phrases of the distortions that you corrected.

Consider the following example:

Suppose a person were once involved in an accident that had caused serious injury to someone else and afterward found that he could not shake off the memory. Suppose that after inspecting the memory closely, he reached a conclusion that his trouble resulted from the fact that he had been denying his part of the responsibility.

He might say to himself, "I have refused to admit that, by failing to look where I was going, I let myself get into a situation that involved danger to myself and others. Yes, the other fellow was at fault, but so was I, even though the law didn't say so."

That piece of honest thinking would have the effect of correcting distortions.

Instead of correcting distortions by bringing up command phrases, it would release them by stating the truth that the command phrases have the effect of contradicting.

Either method of approach to the problem works.

The fact that the distortions are released by stating the truth does not mean that command phrases were absent. Command phrases are always present when distortions are involved. In effect, the command phrases really constitute the wording of the distortions.

In the case cited, perhaps several command phrases would be involved. The following examples suggest their possible nature:

"I'll never admit this was my fault." "Nobody can trap me into saying anything that could hurt me." "I can stay out of trouble by keeping my mouth shut." "I'll never take any chances."

Of course, each of those command phrases has the effect of denying and concealing the truth that it contradicts. Giving attention to the command phrases and seeing how they are illogical and compulsive has the effect of destroying a person's confidence in them, thus allowing him to see the truth that the phrases concealed. Taking a good look at that truth has the effect of forcing those command phrases out of the mind.

The technique of correcting distortions by finding command phrases is easier to use because it has more of an element of indirection in its use. When truth can be faced more directly, the technique of exposing and facing the truth without resort to inspection of the concealing command phrases is fully as effective.

Either way, a single act can correct more than one distortion.

For example, when a piece of truth is contradicted by several distortions, exposing and facing that piece of truth tends to eliminate all the contradicting distortions. When a piece of truth is exposed by giving attention to one command phrase, correction may be gained for every distortion contradicted by that piece of truth.

For the foregoing reasons, distortions can be corrected in

much less time than was required to install them. Whereas they were installed one at a time, they can be corrected in groups. Evidence indicates that quite a large group can be corrected in one operation.

It all depends on the nature of the truth that a person faces.

In the case of the foregoing example, admitting responsibility for his proper share of responsibility for the accident may enable the person to admit responsibility for his share of many other problems and troubles that have nothing to do with that particular accident.

If it does, that is an important result.

The reason is that until responsibility is properly admitted, no person can make the necessary changes in his habits of thought and action so that the dangers involved will not be repeated.

A person who denies responsibility for a mistake thus destroys his ability to correct the thinking that caused his mistake.

The ability to recognize and admit responsibility for mistakes is important to the individual himself, because without it, he cannot free his mind from distortions that compel repetition of mistakes. But it is also important to other people, because it has a startling effect on his ability to get along with them.

II

ONE OF the most frustrating aspects of interpersonal relationships is that people cannot get each other to admit responsibility for the trouble they cause, and usually nothing is gained by trying. Even when the effort succeeds, usually nothing would be gained, and sometimes more trouble erupts.

Nonetheless people ordinarily keep on trying.

A person who freely admits responsibility for his mistakes is a novelty. He has a disarming effect on others, and they display no incentive to attack him.

Usually a person is fearful that if he admits a mistake, something terrible will happen to him. But that fear results from distortions. Unless he has committed some crime or otherwise opened himself to disaster because of what he has done, honest admission is little more than a way of correcting distortions for the person who understands how they operate.

The person who makes the admission is the beneficiary.

He gains advantages that are denied to every person who refuses to make the admission.

III

THE REASON a person refuses to make the admission is not what it seems. Usually people assume that refusal proves an unwillingness to admit, but that is seldom the case. Usually refusal results from his inability to face and admit mistakes because he has not been able to admit to himself the fact that he is responsible.

That is why people tend to blame everything that goes wrong on others.

A person who is victimized by that condition is in trouble. The trouble that results from his mistakes is minor compared with another kind of trouble. The other kind of trouble is that *he is quite completely prevented from learning what he needs to know to manage his life successfully in relation to the various topics of his mental blindness.*

Nobody can tell him anything on those topics.

No doubt you can think of a person in that situation as soon as you try. Perhaps you have been trying for years to tell someone certain things without success. The reason may be that you are trying to get him to admit certain responsibility that he cannot admit because he is mentally blocked and unable to recognize his responsibility.

Just a few command phrases could cause his problem. They might be:

"Nobody is going to get me to admit anything that might put me in a bad light." "If you admit a mistake, the next thing that happens is that you get into trouble." "Nothing is ever my fault, because I'm always careful about what I say and do." The person who has those distortions and lends his conscious support to them is beyond help from anyone who tries to tell him anything that requires his admitting a mistake.

His predicament is much more serious than initially appears evident, which is the case with many kinds of behavior resulting from distortions. Almost literally, he cannot be helped to correct his mistakes. Not by his closest friends or relatives. Not by his employer. Not, in any case, where an admission of responsibility is needed.

Obviously he is going to be involved in many such situations. Everybody is. His only hope is to adopt right intent and get correction for the distortions that destroy his ability to receive the kind of information he needs.

There are two great lessons in the foregoing paragraphs.

The first lesson is that every person might wisely inspect his thinking and his behavior in a search for indications that he cannot admit his mistakes to himself and to others. Just a casual search is not enough. People tend to think they are able to admit their mistakes to themselves; therefore, a deeper search is needed. The matter cannot be settled in one sitting.

Probably the matter cannot be settled without extensive analyses spaced over a period of time. Everybody who makes those analyses gets a series of surprises.

The second lesson is that a person might wisely inspect the persons he deals with most often to determine for himself whether some of them are seriously afflicted in the manner described. Some of them are easily identified.

With others, he may not be able to detect the evidence.

In that case he should wait until the next time a situation arises in which the evidence becomes obvious. He rarely has long to wait. When the situation arises, he will be able to make interesting experiments that may incontrovertibly disclose the proof, though he is not wise to try to force an admission.

No effort to force an admission can succeed unless the person unable to admit his mistakes can be confronted with evidence that has the effect of correcting the interfering distortions.

The reason for that should be obvious from what has been said.

Until the distortions that blind a person to his responsibility are destroyed, his brain is literally incapable of carrying to his conscious awareness any message telling him that he is responsible. On that subject, his brain is blocked and is not functional.

It is not sensible to blame him.

Nobody blames a piece of electronic equipment if it fails to work properly because it is wired up wrong. In effect, that is what is wrong with a person who has distortions. On the subjects of the distortions, his brain is wired up wrong. He caused it to be wired up wrong by doing the thinking that installed the distortions, but once the distortions have been installed, he is helplessly sentenced to carry out the orders of the command phrases.

His only real remedy is to unload his mental circuits, and he is incapable of doing that under any kind of ordinary persuasion or by any other procedure except by the procedure of correcting distortions.

There is much evidence of the truth of that statement.

If ordinary persuasion induced people to change their behavior when controlled by distortions, a spouse would be able to talk his or her spouse out of alcoholism; a counselor would be able to talk addicts out of drugs and related crimes and so on.

Everybody knows that many human problems are virtually impossible to solve.

Because of the impossibility of using persuasion to get an obviously desirable change of mind, people have increasingly turned to medication and other physical procedures to make people tractable. Those procedures are not needed by the person who learns how to correct distortions.

IV

A PERSON who knows how to correct distortions can deal with his ordinary problems just about as fast as they come to his attention. He just needs a willingness to face the truth about them. That puts him in touch with reality on those points.

He cannot get all his changes as fast as he would like.

Whether he realizes it or not, he is forced to deal with his distortions in sequence, although he may correct many command phrases while correcting only one area. He must be patient about his effort to become rational. He spent a long time putting distortions into his mind, and he may have to spend a long time getting them out.

Getting them out, however, is no burden.

As he corrects distortions, he decreases the problems of his life. He corrects them by giving them no more time and attention than he would have to spend dealing with the same problems anyhow. When he corrects distortions, he gets results he could get in no other way.

One result is that by correcting distortions he learns much about the reasons why people are illogical and engage in wrong behavior. He can put that knowledge to good use in his dealings with others.

After he has learned how and why he made a long string of mistakes that he has brought to a halt, he feels more tolerant of other persons who are still making those mistakes. He tends to stop trying to do what cannot be done in his dealings with people, and he starts using new methods that are likely to succeed.

Instead of asking a person to contradict the distortions that cause illogical conversation and behavior, he learns to use two alternative procedures that soon revolutionize his ability to deal successfully with people.

First, he learns to recognize when a person is talking and acting under promptings of his distortions. As a consequence, he allows for whatever is said or done. Second, he learns how to make the corrections of distortions in other persons that are needed to permit successful dealings with them.

He must gain the first of those two abilities before he can gain the second.

Until he has those abilities, he is certain to be frustrated in many of his dealings with people no matter how much he knows about them. All the conventional information on the subject of dealing with people leaves out the knowledge of distortions. Because distortions control a high proportion of everybody's thinking and behavior, that omission is serious.

A person who understands distortions can easily understand human behavior in a way that is beyond the understanding of any expert who does not understand distortions.

By classifying the command phrases under which his friends and relatives and associates operate, he can predict their behavior with remarkable accuracy in various situations. Some of those situations he learns to avoid, and others he learns to manage.

V

WHEN A person sees someone talking and acting under promptings of distortions, he is wise often to ignore what is going on or else allow for it so that he does not contradict the command phrases under restimulation. Contradicting them is nonproductive unless the contradicting is done in such a way that correction of the distortions results.

For that process, both understanding and skill are needed.

Nobody is obligated to assume the task of correcting all the distortions for any of the persons he knows. Obviously that would not be possible so he must be selective. In the beginning he cannot sensibly undertake to correct distortions unless a result is to be gained that somehow aids him in getting relief from trouble.

Often that is the situation.

For example, if your spouse has distortions telling him or her that you are not to be trusted out of sight, you will not have a satisfactory home life until those distortions are corrected. But if your boss has distortions telling him that he must prove himself smarter than any person under him, you will probably do best to let him enjoy the feeling that is so important to him, provided you can accomplish that result without experiencing a serious setback for any of your important objectives.

From the foregoing, it is indicated that the peculiarities of people result from their distortions, and that is correct. A person who had no distortions would always be logical. He would always do the right thing. Presumably no such person exists; therefore, the concept is only theoretical at present.

Perhaps some day such persons will exist.

Until that day comes, you will have to deal with people who have distortions. When command phrases are actuating them, you had better make room for their free expression, or you may get hurt.

The person who realizes that gains an enormous advantage over persons who do not.

The person who does not is in constant danger of getting involved in interpersonal relationships and situations he cannot deal with successfully.

Consider the following examples:

You may have a close relative who has distortions telling

him to start an argument with you at every opportunity. Perhaps the close relative is your brother. Perhaps he installed the distortions in early childhood. In that case there is every likelihood that in childhood you also installed many distortions about your brother. They may tell you that you must rise to every challenge from your brother and must win every one of the arguments he starts. You may also have distortions telling you to lose no opportunity to start arguments with him.

In that situation you and he will often have a bad emotional time whenever you get together.

At first you may suppose that the situation is hopeless and that the only sensible thing to do is to stay away from him. But everybody who has siblings has problems of that sort to a greater or lesser degree. If a person could gather them all in a pile, he would be startled by the size of that pile.

Getting away from your brother would, of course, stop those arguments. But the overwhelming chance is that you also have distortions that have the effect of refusing to let you get away from him. Perhaps you have distortions telling you quite emphatically to get together with your brother at least once a week.

That sort of trouble exists in various ways in every family.

Where distortions of the sort described tend to control family relationships, there will be an enormous amount of useless arguing. If you stop to think of it, you will realize that such is the situation in virtually every family.

The cause might not be the particular combination of distortions cited, but it is a certainty that the cause is distortions.

A person who knows that becomes alert to behavior stimulated by distortions. If he sees useless arguments coming, he manages to evade them. If he sees that one of his close friends or relatives must always have the last word in any discussion, he yields it. If he sees that his close relatives all have to criticize him, he does not try to talk them out of it. If he sees that one of his friends cannot talk about some particular subject without getting excited, he leaves that subject out of the conversation.

After he has learned to recognize conversation and behavior that results from promptings by distortions, he is in a position to avoid many otherwise difficult situations. But sometimes he cannot avoid those situations.

Consider the following examples of that sort:

Suppose a husband is unable to discuss money with his wife, actually cannot mention the subject, which is the case in many families. Suppose that every discussion about finances causes an immediate emotional outburst that literally prevents the husband from saying what he considers necessary.

That is a problem he cannot easily sidestep.

Suppose the wife cannot get her husband to listen when she discusses what to do about the children. That kind of difficulty is widespread, and it can result from a single distortion installed in a moment of anger. Perhaps the command phrase might be "I'll never give those rascals another moment of my attention!" Then suppose the children have serious difficulties of one kind or another.

Unless she understands distortions and the problems and trouble they cause, she is in a serious predicament. She can say words to her husband; he can seem to be listening, but he cannot put his mind on what she says.

That is a problem she cannot easily sidestep.

Those examples are not farfetched. Millions of husbands and wives are in that sort of predicament, not just in relation to money matters and their children but in relation to various other topics.

It is not difficult to see the evidence of such trouble.

Even if a reader does not know a married couple in the predicament described, probably you can think of some person who habitually refuses or fails to listen to you. Perhaps his refusal or failure relates to certain topics, as when he refuses or fails to hear anything you say about your job, your concerns or your travel plans. Perhaps the person's refusal or failure to listen relates to virtually everything you say.

If that person is important to you, that is a problem you may not be able to ignore.

In that case you had better learn how to make corrections of distortions in other persons when those corrections are needed to permit your dealing successfully with them.

VI

BEFORE YOU start correcting distortions in someone else, sincerely try to correct your own distortions that might also contribute to the problems and trouble you are trying to eliminate.

Where any kind of conflict is involved, you can be sure there are distortions on both sides.

A person who is wholly logical somehow manages to avoid conflict. Of course, that statement, at first, may seem to be unjustified by just about everybody who happens to be engaged in a conflict. When a person really understands distortions, he discovers that there is always a way out of every invitation to conflict.

Consider the following example:

Suppose a person occasionally feels unhappy about favoritism shown one of his brothers or sisters by their mother. That is a common situation that causes an enormous amount of emotional distress in families.

In many cases the mother cannot see virtues in the child who is not favored and cannot see faults in the child who is.

Of course, the mother has distortions, too.

A person who does not understand distortions may spend much of his childhood and adult life in a futile effort to win favor from his mother. If he is broadly rejected, he never succeeds. Or when he succeeds selectively, the favor is given reluctantly. Because the seeming need for a certain amount of favor is strong, his effort never really stops.

The person who seeks favor probably does not know that he is seeking it, because the promptings of distortions are largely unconscious. If he carefully studies his conversation and behavior, he can detect his effort, and when he does, he is in a position to release the distortions responsible for it. Prior to that, he is merely actuated by those distortions.

All during the years when the distortions actuate him, he suffers from a longing desire to win favor he cannot get. As a result of his desire, he wants to change his mother's thinking, but if he begins to inspect his thinking properly, he uncovers many distortions that have controlled him on that subject.

Many of those distortions were installed in his moments of rebellion over the fact that his mother's favors went to his rival. Nevertheless they are distortions. They result not so much from the fact that he was mistreated, although it is perhaps true that he was mistreated, as from the fact that his reaction to the treatment was one of rebellion.

When he discovers that he has such distortions, he should make the effort to correct them.

He is wise to do that before he attempts to change his mother's thinking. Until he does, he cannot clearly see and understand the problem he is dealing with because his distortions alter his judgment. His command phrases blind him to certain aspects of the problem, and they cause him to suppose he sees certain other aspects of the problem that may be merely products of his imagination.

Those command phrases could be the following:

"She never pays any attention to me." "He never does anything wrong in her eyes." "I'll make her listen to me." "If I try hard enough, I can make her agree that I'm a better son than he is." "I have to make her love me the most."

Command phrases of that kind can cause great misery. If you happen to have those phrases, you will benefit enormously by recognizing them for what they are and getting rid of them. After that, you will feel very different in your attitude toward your mother.

If she is available, she will also notice the difference.

The great probability is that you will notice a marked change in her attitude toward you, just because of the change in you. If not, hesitate a little longer.

Before you try to correct the distortions in her, ask yourself whether the result is worth seeking. Perhaps you will realize that you have gained so much stability by destroying your emotional dependency on your mother's approval that you will want to delay taking the next step until you can analyze the new situation.

VII

IT IS a little-noted fact that people are so dependent on one another emotionally that, in many situations, they are incapable of taking independent action.

That is an unfortunate state of affairs. A person who is incapable of taking independent action is a person whose brains are in chains.

Emotional dependency on another person destroys his ability to be intelligent about that person. In any situation where the emotional relationship is crucial to any action he might take, he is incapable of being intelligent about that action.

Therefore, he should get free of emotional dependencies.

They are all a matter of command phrases, and many of them are difficult to find, because the dependency seems logical to the person who installed the phrases.

The following sentences are typical examples:

"I can't decide until I find out what Mother thinks." "If my mother disapproves of this, I'll have to give up the whole idea." "Nobody can separate me from my mother, even for a minute." "Mother's the only one who understands me."

Similar command phrases may relate to persons other

than a mother. They may relate to close relatives or a close friend. They are likely to relate to one's boss, and the more emotional experiences a person has gone through in relation to his boss, the more likely he or she is to have a large collection of distortions making him emotionally dependent on the boss.

It is important that every kind of emotional dependency is noticed and given proper attention. Why? Because it has its roots in distortions and, therefore, causes thinking on the subjects of the distortions to be illogical and wrong. The distortions reduce the chance to satisfy what is presumed to be the purpose of the relationship.

At first some persons are afraid to destroy emotional relationships. They are afraid they may not like the consequences. The evidence is that those fears are groundless.

It is true that when distortions are corrected people's dealings with friends and relatives undergo many profound changes. The average person can think of many ways he would like those dealings to change.

He has no sound reason to fear any right change.

Very likely he does not get all the changes he thinks in advance he would like to get. Some of those changes are not in everybody's best interests. If he got them, they would cause more trouble instead of getting him out of trouble and, therefore, would not be desirable. As he progresses, he improves his thinking.

Consider the following example:

At first he may wish to produce changes that would enable him to prove to someone else that he is a person of very unusual ability who is being misunderstood and abused.

Presently he may see that a wish of that sort is illogical.

In the process of seeing that, he comes to realize that what the other person thinks of him makes less difference than he had earlier supposed. He may even decide that he doesn't care. He surely will decide that if the other person has a wrong impression, it is more the other person's problem than his. After all, the person with the wrong impression is the person whose thinking has gone astray.

What changes a person will actually desire to make after correcting his own distortions, he cannot successfully decide in advance. They tend to be changes he wants to make because he sees their benefit. Until he corrects his own distortions directly affecting a given relationship, he is in danger of seeking changes that he might later have reason to regret.

After he corrects his distortions regarding his relationship with another person, the overwhelming likelihood is that he finds he no longer has problems in that relationship.

He finds that he no longer cares about the opinions that had previously annoyed him. He finds that the fact of not caring causes a complete change in those opinions. He finds that behavior that formerly annoyed him not only causes no more annoyance but actually causes him to feel sorry for the person he formerly had blamed. He finds that he becomes able to avoid entanglements of many kinds that he had found objectionable in the past.

If so, he naturally wants to extend that progress.

He will want to destroy all the emotional dependencies he still possesses so that he can make all those relationships impersonal and right.

The value of impersonal relationships, at first, may be difficult for many persons to understand; therefore, the subject will be given attention. In order to explain what is meant, certain liberties with definitions are taken.

A personal relationship is defined as a relationship in which thinking is colored by friendliness and/or animosity. A person realizes at once that virtually all relationships are so colored, but few persons have any idea of the hazardous consequences.

Those consequences are stated next.

A friendly personal relationship tends to blind a person

to all the faults in the person toward whom friendliness is felt. It tends to cause faults to appear as virtues perhaps. On the other hand, an unfriendly attitude tends to blind a person to all the virtues of the person toward whom the unfriendliness is felt. It tends to cause his virtues often to appear as faults.

The mental blindness resulting from a friendly or unfriendly personal relationship impairs the ability of the person who feels the friendliness or unfriendliness to be intelligent about the way he handles the relationship.

He overlooks faults or virtues, or he sees faults or virtues where they do not exist. Therefore, he depends on his friends in ways in which they may not be reliable; consequently they disappoint him. Also he refuses to depend on persons he dislikes in ways that they would prove wholly reliable if he did.

In either case, he gets a wrong result.

There is a certain fallacy in popular thinking that causes people to make the mistake of depending on people when they should not. The fallacy is based on the often-repeated statement that everybody should look for the good in persons he knows and overlook the bad. That advice can easily lead to self-delusion.

If a person insists on blinding himself to facts, he may suffer when those facts unexpectedly cause some trouble.

VIII

AN IMPERSONAL relationship is not devoid of friendliness. It is a relationship that is devoid of unnatural and illogical dependencies on personal judgments. It is a relationship that is devoid of incorrect interpretations of personal values of the sort that are most likely to be misunderstood.

It is a relationship based on correct information instead of unreal fantasies.

A person who seeks impersonal relationships to prevent troubles from developing soon realizes that everything wrong about the conversation and behavior of persons he knows is caused by distortions. *He also realizes that what is wrong about his acquaintances is not able to hurt him or his interests unless he lets it. More important, he learns how he can prevent himself from suffering as a result of anything said or done by someone else.*

He learns what some people have sensed is true but have not been able to establish successfully in a workable behavioral code.

He learns that nobody can hurt him except himself.

Therefore, he loses his incentive to try to solve his problems by trying to change the behavior of other people. He develops incentives to solve his problems by changing himself. He learns that the way to change himself is not to try to change himself but to correct the distortions that cause him to behave as he does.

That helps to set him free from other people's problems.

He becomes able to adopt an impersonal attitude completely free from emotional dependencies toward every person with whom he deals, but that takes time. Meanwhile he gets into one situation after another that he dislikes. If he remembers not to react in emotional rebellion but to correct the distortions that direct his thinking into areas of unreality, he successfully avoids many serious problems and prevents much trouble.

In some situations he must attempt to change the behavior of someone who is behaving badly, even if only because he has not yet corrected enough of his own distortions to understand what is going on.

There is another reason why he might need to influence someone else toward rational behavior.

Perhaps his spouse or other person close to him is in trouble and needs help. If so, he is limited in the kind of help he can give. He helps most easily the person in trouble who understands distortions. In that case he can talk in terms of command phrases and expect that his efforts will meet with a display of real cooperation.

A husband and wife who both understand distortions can easily do very wonderful things in helping each other to release themselves from bondage to wrong thinking.

All the information they really need has already been stated.

But in various situations, the person who needs help may be a person who knows nothing about distortions and does not want to learn. Or perhaps he is someone who has been given that information and rejected it.

Even for those persons, distortions can be corrected.

IX

A **PERSON *corrects a distortion when he faces the truth that the distortion conceals. Usually he cannot do that unless he willingly seeks the truth.*** Even then, he cannot do it directly, so he must understand how to make an indirect approach. That is easily accomplished if he infers the command phrases from the conversation, behavior, his emotional state or from some other indirect indication.

Success, in that case, depends on voluntary cooperation.

Nobody can be compelled to offer voluntary cooperation. Therefore, nobody can be compelled to avail himself of the help offered by use of the procedures described in this book.

But in certain situations, the help can be forced on him.

The reason it can be forced on him is not that the need to face truth can be obviated. Instead, it is that the act of facing truth can be made coercive.

That is what is sometimes needed. When it is, no other procedure can take its place.

Probably everybody, at various times in his life, has wanted to know how he could compel a change in someone else's behavior. Virtually everybody has been frustrated in various situations of that sort. On occasion, the average person has resorted to coercion that is physical in nature, without getting the desired result.

There is a solid reason why physical coercion fails.

The reason is that it cannot induce voluntary action. You can compel a person to act by forcing him, but after you turn your back, he reverts to doing as he pleases. ***You can apply painful physical force if you are big enough and strong enough, but you can't compel him to change his thinking.***

He has to do that himself.

If he ought to change his thinking, the only reason he fails or refuses is that he doesn't know why he should.

The reason he should is that he has failed or refused to face a piece of truth, a situation of reality. Therefore, compelling him to face that piece of truth describing the reality has the effect of causing him to decide to change his thinking.

The situation can easily be illustrated.

Suppose you want a person to move six feet away from where he is standing, because unless he moves quickly, he will be killed by a fast-approaching truck. You may have difficulty getting him to take orders from you, but he will respect the approaching truck. All that is needed is to call it to his attention in such a way that he cannot resist getting the information that apprises him of his predicament.

He does the rest.

The moving truck represents a piece of reality. If he had seen that piece of reality himself, he would have acted in accord with it. The same is true of any other piece of reality that is concealed by distortions of logic.

Reveal that piece of reality.

All that is necessary is to state the appropriate truth in sufficiently descriptive terms that the corresponding reality cannot be ignored. The immediate result is that every distortion that contradicts that particular piece of reality is given instantaneous and effective contradiction. The urge to persist in the irrational behavior is suddenly replaced by an impulse to scramble into a position of safety.

Accuracy is needed, and, at first, the degree of accuracy is difficult to understand. It is greater than that of a sharpshooter who gets credit for a perfect shot if he hits inside the edge of a bull's-eye. In this instance no leeway is permissible because no approximation permits a successful change.

The foregoing procedure does not correct distortions of logic for the person who is still intent on getting his way. Rather, it enables him to act in contradiction to distortions in his search for self-protection.

It is virtually impossible for a person who does not understand distortions of logic to make real corrections by accident. It can be done, although the procedure opposes virtually every seemingly natural inclination. With enough understanding, corrections can occasionally be forced, even against opposition from a person who does not understand and, therefore, resists.

Total precision of approach is required.

Information previously presented will serve as a basis for correct understanding of the proper approach if carefully considered. The appropriate information relates to the procedure for correcting a distortion by recognizing the exact words of the command phrase that contains the distortion.

Even if the words were formulated forty years earlier in some foreign language that the victim of the phrase no longer consciously understands, the command phrase may have only one possible wording. That is the wording which precisely captures the thinking that was done at the time when the distortion was installed.

The slightest variation in those words could cause a failure to produce the desired correction.

Earlier it was said that in addition to considering the words of the command phrase, another form of the technique for correcting a distortion is to disclose the truth concealed by the command phrase. That is what is done when you state that truth to a person you are trying to help, but the truth must be stated just as exactly as the command phrase. It cannot be merely a statement of some truth that the command phrase happens to contradict.

It must be the exact statement.

If the exact statement happens to contradict more than one distortion, many distortions thus contradicted may be corrected. But that cannot happen unless an exact contradiction of one of the distortions is involved in the statement of truth.

The reason this topic is given emphasis is that failure to produce the exact statement of truth may cause the person you are trying to help to become infuriated.

Anything you tell him that haphazardly contradicts one of his distortions is totally unacceptable to him. Even though what you say seems to have meaning so obvious it cannot be missed, he will miss it. So long as he retains the distortion concealing the truth, he simply is unable to comprehend that truth. Trying to tell him what he cannot comprehend and once determinedly hid from himself arouses strong emotion that will be aimed at you.

Statement of the exact truth that is contradicted by a distortion avoids that effect.

At first glance the reason is startling.

The reason is that no one can simultaneously retain both untruth and truth on exactly the same topic. Could he believe that it is noon after he has learned that it is midnight? Truth forces untruth out because truth uses the same mental circuits that must be used to retain the untruth.

It is as though a person has both arms loaded with a large package and is then tossed another package that he must catch. Necessarily he drops the package he already holds.

A listener cannot hear and comprehend the simple meaning of words of precise truth that he has tried to hide by adoption of an untruth without dropping the untruth. Since the distortion of logic is contained in the untruth, he drops the distortion.

He drops it whether he knows what is happening or not.

X

ALTHOUGH THE statement of truth must be exact, there is an easy way to find it. There may be millions of statements of truth that are true and have the effect of contradicting the distortion to be corrected, but there is an easy way to select exactly the one statement of truth that applies.

The easy way is not found accidentally.

If that were possible, people would have been able to solve their difficult human problems long ago.

Certainly people have long been able to detect illogical behavior in each other. They have often been able to point out how the behavior is wrong, but everything they say tends to restimulate the distortions responsible for it without correcting them. Therefore, everything they say is likely to cause emotional blowups and do more harm than good.

That is because people fail to say what contradicts the distortions exactly. When they learn how, they can begin to succeed in solving difficult interpersonal problems.

The key is found in the command phrase of the distortion to be corrected. The exact statement of truth is precisely opposite to the wording of the command phrase of the distortion.

Therefore, do not seek the truth directly.

First, get the command phrase. Then ask yourself what is exactly opposite to it in meaning. That is the precise piece of truth to tell the person you are trying to help.

Chapter 7

Take Your Brains Out of Chains

WHILE GIVING someone the piece of truth that makes him free of a distortion of logic, you need not shout. You need not speak with emphasis. You need only state the words audibly and correctly at a time when the other person is actually listening.

He cannot help throwing the proper mental switches.

The purpose of shouting might be to intimidate the person you are trying to help. Even if he is subject to intimidation, the shouting is notoriously ineffective. When it seems effective, it is not that understanding has been achieved. It is that intimidation has overpowered resistance.

If the correct piece of precise truth is stated in softly spoken words, the information penetrates. Appropriate mental switches are thrown, and a change of thinking results. The listener sees the light of reason and acts on it.

It is as though a miracle has occurred.

One result is that he gets his brains out of chains. However, that is not the only result. An additional result is that you also get your brains out of chains. You no longer feel tied down to the hopeless task of trying to change the thinking of a person who seems bent on refusing to change it, no matter what you say.

The resulting release from mental and emotional burdens can be very great. Perhaps you have expended a large part of your time and energy trying unsuccessfully to deal with certain problems of persuasion that are important to you. Or perhaps you have failed to deal with problems of that sort and have, therefore, adjusted your life to the failure at considerable sacrifice.

If so, you have a technique to set yourself free.

At first you may have difficulty seeing how to apply the technique. Until you know how to detect command phrases, the technique has no value to you. Even after you know how to detect command phrases, your first attempts to use the technique may fail. But ultimate results are such that persistence will be rewarded.

Next, the technique will be illustrated.

Suppose you have to deal with an associate who insists that he should never get any difficult piece of work to do and who contrives to get every piece of difficult work done by someone else. As a result, you are likely to have trouble with that person.

If he understands distortions, he can solve the problem himself. In that case he does so as soon as he becomes aware of it. In any case, you may be able to help him.

Assume that you have identified the command phrase.

For purposes of illustration, the command phrase might be, "Whenever I try anything difficult, I fail."

If he understands and accepts the explanation of distortions, telling him that command phrase would cause an immediate correction. But if he does not understand nor accept the theory, telling him that command phrase might induce either of two dishonest reactions.

First, he might deny that he ever harbored such a thought. If so, his denial prevents a correction. Second, he might agree with the command phrase.

"Yes," he may say, "that's exactly what happens!"

If so, his difficulty is that he believes the command phrase and, therefore, supports it. He cannot be released from further domination by a command phrase until he finds some reason for disagreeing with it.

Unless he withdraws his support for the wrong thought, he tends to go on justifying his behavior and continuing it until the domination is broken.

Therefore, you must do more than tell him the phrase. Conceivably you could tell him, "You're always trying to get your difficult work done by others." That, you can be assured, he will resent. He won't believe it. The reason he won't believe it is that the motive that causes him to get his difficult work done by others is an unconscious motive which originates in his distortion. He just does not recognize what he is doing clearly enough to understand it, and he cannot know about his unconscious motive.

If you could successfully tell him the command phrase and induce him to accept it as such, that would make his unconscious motive conscious. It would enable him to detect the fact that his motive is illogical, and he would abandon it at once without urging from you.

For purposes of this example, that is what you cannot do.

Perhaps you will cast about for other ways of getting your point across. There is only one way that works, and it cannot be found unless you are specifically looking for it.

To find that way, start reasoning from the command phrase.

If the command phrase is "Whenever I try anything difficult, I fail," you might get somewhere by using those words and following them with an explanation. Then add a general contradiction. For example, "You think that whenever you try anything difficult you fail, but really that isn't true. There have been times I've seen you try difficult things and succeed."

If he is reasonably tractable, that remark may cause a correction of the distortion. But if he is not reasonably tractable, he may react to the first part of your sentence by agreeing with it so very vehemently that he doesn't even hear the second part.

You may find success by experimenting with that procedure, and you will be able to start more easily than with the procedure of making an exact contradiction of the command phrase.

In order to make the exact contradiction, you must have the ability to think from a concept to its exact opposite.

II

THE EXACT opposite is not always what it seems. For example, in this case it is *not* "Whenever I try anything difficult, I won't fail." That is only another contradiction of the sort that would be likely to arouse resistance.

That is not what is needed.

A distortion is always exactly opposite to the truth which it contradicts. It is the contradicted truth that is needed.

If you ask inside yourself for the contradicted truth, assuming that you have no distortions on the subject involved, the words tend to come into your mind. Those words may startle you. In fact, they may startle you enough that you are tempted to reject them.

For example, the exact opposite of the phrase under discussion is "Whenever I try anything difficult, I succeed."

To an incautious person those words might seem preposterous.

The correction of those words can be understood by a person who realizes that logical action always succeeds, that a person who is really logical, therefore, does not fail, and that a person who is afflicted by the specified command phrase would not be trying to do something difficult but would actually be trying to fail, for the simple reason that such is his unconscious prompting.

Additional light can be shed by another realization.

Because of distortions, people seldom actually try to do just what they assume they are trying to do. For example, a scientist who assumes that he is trying to find a cure for cancer might, in fact, have command phrases causing him to be trying instead to become rich and famous as the person who found the cure. That would cause him to be frustrated, because it would destroy his ability to put his mind directly on the problem that he imagines he is trying to solve.

If that scientist as a child installed a command phrase saying "Whenever I try anything difficult, I fail," he is certain to have a tendency to be guided by it. But if he corrects that distortion or lets it be corrected for him by someone else, he then becomes more nearly able to do exactly what he supposed he was attempting. He may still fail to gain the desired success, but not because of that command phrase. It is true that a person who is really trying to do exactly what he thinks he is trying to do has a way of succeeding.

The foregoing information can be condensed into a sentence that gets results under the conditions specified. That sentence might be "Whenever you try anything difficult, you succeed, and, therefore, you ought to start trying." The first part of the sentence corrects the distortion that it contradicts exactly, and it also corrects every other distortion that it contradicts directly enough. Even before the remainder of the sentence can be expressed, it accomplishes the correction of those distortions instantly. It meets with no resistance because the resistance has already been destroyed.

The desired result appears as if by magic.

Sometimes the appearance of the result can be impeded by bad handling of the procedure. Suppose, for example, that you do not use the procedure until after you have already made a dozen unsuccessful efforts to change the other person's thinking on the subject of the distortion. In that case he has already gone on record with denials and refusals. Even though he is enabled to see the light of truth and become logical on the subject of the distortion, he naturally feels that he cannot go back on his earlier statements.

Therefore, you get a delayed reaction.

You may not be able to get him to accept the particular piece of difficult work over which he rebelled, but you should be able to get him to accept similar work thereafter.

III

NEXT COMES a delicate subject, and it is quite important for you to understand that subject. Unless you do, you will not be able to use the technique under discussion.

It is the subject of the motives that make you want to use it.

If you are like most persons, you can think of several friends and relatives you would like to change. Why? If your motive is to help them get out of trouble, you may succeed. But if your motive is to adapt them to your personal wishes, you will fail.

You cannot make any improper use of the technique.

The basic reason is that using truth to get a wrong result is impossible. That may sound pious, but, in reality, it is practical common sense. And it is certainly correct.

People get into trouble by trying to abuse truth. They cannot get out of trouble until they abandon that effort.

How can you be sure of abandoning it?

Ask yourself whether you think your reason for wanting to change another person is really honest. If it is, you may be on the right track. Then ask yourself whether you are really unemotional about the effort you intend to make. Unless you are, back away.

The presence of emotion shows that there is still something wrong with your motivation.

Under analysis, you will probably recognize that your emotion results from some sort of feeling that the other person is somehow causing you trouble you would like him to stop. That feeling is evidence of a motive that clouds your judgment and inhibits your proper use of the technique.

Before you can proceed satisfactorily, you must be able

to base your action on right motivation. How can you tell when you are ready to do that? At first you may not be able to tell. However, when you find yourself about to approach the problem without emotion, perhaps you are ready. If you are ready, you will succeed.

Your freedom from emotion will free enough of your intelligence that you can perceive the truth to be stated. It will allow you to present that truth without inviting conflict.

When you can meet those specifications, you can do wonders in an effort to help people effectuate changes, even against their resistance.

IV

THE ADVANTAGE of the foregoing technique in dealing with troublesome situations is difficult to exaggerate. So great is that advantage that even if you must fumble with the technique over a period of months before you learn it, you will find it worth the effort.

By attempting to use it, you make many discoveries.

You discover that a difficult person is really not a person who is peculiarly obnoxious. He is simply a person who has fixed, inflexible ideas that he formed in his moments of rebellious, emotional thinking and who is trapped by the resulting command phrases.

You will learn that a person who is wrong cannot avoid being wrong. You will learn that blaming a person who is wrong is futile, that people are often wrong when they do not know they are wrong, and that they insist on their rightness most vigorously when it is wholly imaginary.

What you learn will help to set your faculties free.

Perhaps the subtlest kind of slavery is slavery to distortions. A person who does not understand distortions is not only a slave to his own distortions, but, in a certain sense, he is a slave to everybody's.

He takes seriously what he would disregard if he realized it was the product of a mind that, in effect, is wired up wrong. He tries to change people's thinking when because of distortions it cannot be changed. He reacts to illogical conversation and wrong behavior by getting himself into many disagreeable situations that he could avoid.

His slavery to his own distortions is more serious.

Every distortion gives him a false concept by which to live. What is more important, it deprives him of the correct concept on the same point.

What he needs is a kind of brainwashing.

Not the brainwashing that puts thinking into his mind, but a brainwashing that washes out all his wrong thinking. He can get that brainwashing in only one way: correcting distortions of logic. It will improve matters more than he or anyone else could imagine in advance.

Nevertheless at first a person may resist.

He would rather die than face the pieces of truth and reality he must face to become free. But unless he faces them, he keeps his problems and stays in trouble.

V

EVERY DISTORTION involves the risk of death for the person. There are various ways of stating the risk, but most of them cannot be understood without a fairly substantial amount of experience in dealing with many different kinds of distortions.

Therefore, only one statement is presented.

From what has gone before, it is clear that every distortion has an effect of depriving its victim of his ability to be logical on the subject of the distortion. In other words, it impairs his effective intelligence and deprives him of the use of some of his brainpower.

How can he be sure that he will not someday need that

particular portion of his logic, his intelligence and his brainpower in order to save his life?

He can't.

At first a person is totally unaware of that fact. Until he learns about distortions and how they work, he has no way of knowing that he has suffered any loss of logic and intelligence and brainpower.

He knows others have something wrong with them.

He may tell people that everybody else is crazy, but somehow it escapes his detection that what applies to other people just might happen to apply to him, too.

When he understands distortions, he realizes not only what is wrong with everybody else but also that he suffers from exactly the same affliction. He does not regard that as bad news. If he understands it, he regards it as good news. It puts him on the road toward startling improvements.

Every time he corrects a distortion, he restores lost faculties. Thereafter he can use those faculties productively. He is able to be in touch with reality which gives him the use of intelligence he was deprived of as long as he had the distortions.

In his daily life he accumulates enormous benefits as he learns how to deal with situations that formerly had left him frustrated and impotent.

Increasingly he gets his brains out of chains.